# CONTENTS

# ACRONYMS

| | |
|---|---|
| AFRICOM | United States Africa Command |
| ADS | USAID Automated Directives System |
| AO | Agreement Officer |
| AOR | Agreement Officer Representative |
| CDCS | Country Development and Cooperation Strategy |
| CENTCOM | United States Central Command |
| CEO | Chief Executive Officer |
| CO | Contracting Officer |
| COCOMS | Combatant Commands |
| COR | Contracting Officer Representative |
| CSE | Commercial Sexual Exploitation |
| CSO | Civil Society Organization |
| CSR | Corporate Social Responsibility |
| C–TIP | Counter-Trafficking in Persons |
| DCHA | USAID Bureau for Democracy, Conflict and Humanitarian Assistance |
| DHS | United States Department of Homeland Security |
| DRG | Center of Excellence on Democracy, Human Rights and Governance (USAID) |
| DO | Development Objective |
| DOD | United States Department of Defense |
| DOJ | United States Department of Justice |
| DOL | United States Department of Labor |
| DOS | United States Department of State |
| ED | United States Department of Education |
| EEOC | United States Equal Employment Opportunity Commission |
| E&E | USAID Bureau for Europe and Eurasia |
| FAI | Federal Acquisition Institute |

| | |
|---|---|
| FAR | Federal Acquisition Regulation |
| FY | Fiscal Year |
| GCLMS | Government of Ghana Child Labor Monitoring Systems |
| GRETA | Council of Europe's Group of Experts on Action against Trafficking in Human Beings |
| HHS | United States Department of Health and Human Services |
| ICE | United States Immigration and Customs Enforcement |
| ICITAP | International Criminal Investigative Training Assistance Program (DOJ) |
| ICMPD | International Center for Migration Policy Development |
| IDEA | Office of Innovation & Development Alliances (USAID) |
| IDP | Internally Displaced Person |
| IHR | Institute of Human Rights |
| ILAB | United States Department of Labor, Bureau of International Labor Affairs |
| ILO | International Labour Organization |
| IOM | International Organization for Migration |
| IQC | Indefinite Quantity Contract |
| IR | Intermediate Results |
| J/TIP | United States Department of State, Office to Combat and Monitor Trafficking in Persons |
| LIA | Legislative Impact Analysis |
| MARPs | Most At-Risk Populations |
| M&E | Monitoring & Evaluation |
| ME&L | Monitoring, Evaluation and Learning |
| MTV EXIT | Music Television End Exploitation and Trafficking Foundation |
| NGO | Non-Governmental Organization |
| NAP | National Action Plan |
| NRM | National Referral Mechanism |
| OIG | USAID Office of Inspector General |
| OPDAT | Overseas Prosecutorial Development, Assistance and Training Program (DOJ) |
| OSCE | Organization for Security and Cooperation in Europe |
| PEB | Procurement Executive Bulletin |

| | |
|---|---|
| PITF | President's Interagency Task Force to Monitor and Combat Trafficking |
| PPD6 | Presidential Policy Directive 6 on Global Development (2010) |
| PPL | USAID Bureau for Policy, Planning and Learning |
| PPP | Public-Private Partnerships |
| PRM | U.S. Department of State Bureau of Population, Refugees, and Migration |
| QDDR | Quadrennial Diplomacy and Development Review |
| SEE | South-East Europe |
| SPOG | Senior Policy Operating Group |
| SOCOM | United States Special Operations Command |
| SOP | Standard Operating Procedure |
| TIP | Trafficking in Persons |
| TRM | Transnational Referral Mechanism |
| TVPA | Trafficking Victims Protection Act |
| TVPRA | Trafficking Victims Protection Reauthorization Act |
| UK | United Kingdom |
| UN.GIFT | United Nations Global Initiative to Fight Human Trafficking |
| UNICEF | United Nations Children's Fund |
| UNODC | United Nations Office on Drugs and Crime |
| USAID | United States Agency for International Development |
| USDA | United States Department of Agriculture |
| USG | United States Government |
| VoT | Victim of Trafficking |

# EXECUTIVE SUMMARY

Trafficking in persons (TIP) is a global crime that involves the "recruitment, transportation, transfer, harbouring or receipt of persons" through the use of force, fraud, or coercion for the purposes of exploitation. A modern form of slavery, human trafficking constitutes a violation of human rights in which victims are deprived of their humanity and basic freedom. TIP can involve either sex or labor exploitation, or both.[1]

Human traffickers earn an estimated $32 billion annually in profits, just under the amount earned through arms and narcotics trafficking.[2] People are enslaved in circumstances of sex and/or labor exploitation all around the world, including in the United States. Quantifying the scale of human trafficking is challenging, in part due to the difficulty of collecting accurate data on this clandestine trade. As of June 2012, the International Labour Organization estimated that 20.9 million people are enslaved in sex or labor exploitation.[3]

TIP is linked to numerous development and security issues, including the prominence of transnational organized crime, ineffective legal protections, health threats, insufficient labor standards and enforcement, lackluster economic development, gender and ethnic discrimination, and poor migration policies and practices. Since 2002, there has been a proliferation of national, regional, and international regulatory frameworks to combat TIP. However, enforcement of these agreements and obligations has been uneven.[4] Multiple actors—international governmental and non-governmental organizations, domestic governments, civil society, media, the private sector, and perhaps most important, consumers around the world—need to commit to countering TIP in order for the legal and regulatory frameworks to have full impact.

To be a catalytic partner in growing this movement, the United States Agency for International Development (USAID) issued its Counter-Trafficking in Persons (C–TIP) Policy in February 2012.[5] Additionally, it has programmed approximately $179.9 million in C–TIP activities in 68 countries and Regional Missions worldwide between FY 2001-FY 2011. USAID has worked on average in 20-25 countries per year on programs to combat trafficking.[6] In 2011, USAID provided $16.6 million to combat human trafficking in 25 countries. The majority of that funding went to Tier Two and Tier Two Watch List countries.

This new Counter-Trafficking in Persons Field Guide is designed as a practical resource for USAID officers to help implement the C–TIP Policy. It complements the full body of technical tools providing Agency-specific guidance to USAID personnel on how to program United States Government (USG) resources, including recommendations for integrating C–TIP components into existing programs, options

---

[1] The Palermo Protocol: available at:
http://www.uncjin.org/Documents/Conventions/dcatoc/final_documents_2/convention_%20traff_eng.pdf.

[2] International Labour Organization (ILO). 2008. *Forced Labour and Human Trafficking: Handbook for Labour Inspectors.* Geneva, Switzerland, 7.

[3] ILO. 2012. "Global Estimates of Forced Labour Factsheet." Geneva, Switzerland, June.

[4] Enforcement will likely emerge from a mix of compliance mechanisms (e.g. threatening sanctions and clear consequences) and normative change that challenges societal attitudes, currently relatively complacent regarding this phenomenon. As a truly global movement to combat trafficking grows, agreements and obligations should be invoked with greater regularity.

[5] "USAID Counter Trafficking In Persons Policy," February 2012, http://pdf.usaid.gov/pdf_docs/PDACT111.pdf.

[6] Between FY 2001-FY 2010, USAID provided 22% of USG C–TIP international programming with the remainder provided by the United States Department of (DOS) and Department of Labor (DOL).

for stand-alone C–TIP initiatives, and suggestions on monitoring and evaluating the impact of specific programming interventions. In addition, this Guide emphasizes the importance of uniting all stakeholders and consolidating efforts into a comprehensive C–TIP movement. Additional tools and information regarding counter-trafficking and implementation of the Policy are available at http://www.usaid.gov/trafficking and USAID's ProgramNet site.

# PART I. USAID COUNTERING TRAFFICKING IN PERSONS POLICY

The 2012 C–TIP Policy is a direct response to the fact that TIP is a massive development problem affecting millions of men, women, and children. This new Policy also reflects the large body of law that has emerged in the last several decades to combat this crime. It incorporates the principles set forth in the Victims of Trafficking and Violence Protection Act of 2000, and subsequent reauthorizations (collectively TVPA).[7] It adheres to the standards in the United Nations Protocol to Prevent, Suppress and Punish Trafficking in Persons, Especially Women and Children, supplementing the United Nations Convention against Transnational Organized Crime (the "Palermo Protocol" or "the Protocol").[8] Finally, it is inspired by the Thirteenth Amendment to the U.S. Constitution prohibiting slavery and involuntary servitude and reflects the standards of international anti-slavery law. The Policy is informed by the "Prevention, Protection, Prosecution, and Partnership paradigm" (4Ps paradigm).

*Prevention:* Education about trafficking for vulnerable populations, for employers whose business practices may facilitate or constitute trafficking, and for first responders in a position to identify and help rescue or support trafficking victims, such as social workers, health care professionals, police, and humanitarian aid staff is a fundamental part of prevention. Interventions include economic and other activities that create an environment in which TIP cannot prosper. These programs address the conditions that allow trafficking to flourish, such as lack of viable economic or educational opportunities, gender and ethnic discrimination, corruption, and weak governance and rule of law. Prevention interventions promote a growing awareness of trafficking in both the formal and informal labor markets and an increased need for transparency and monitoring in product supply chains.

*Protection:* The protection of trafficked persons is the cornerstone of a victim-centered approach. International standards, including the Palermo Protocol, encourage States to provide care for trafficked persons, including shelter, security, access to a broad range of services and, where appropriate, immigration relief.[9] Protection programs focus on the identification of trafficked persons and the development of national and regional referral mechanisms that ensure survivors are provided shelter, food, counseling, legal assistance, as well as repatriation or reintegration services.

*Prosecution:* The low rate of TIP prosecutions and convictions worldwide indicates a need for increased efforts to obtain justice for victims and to punish perpetrators. According to DOS TIP Global Law Enforcement Data, the number of trafficking prosecutions and convictions is significantly smaller than the number of victims identified and miniscule compared to the estimated number of TIP victims. For example, the International Labour Organization (ILO) estimated as of 2012 that approximately 20.9

---

[7]Victims of Trafficking and Violence Protection Act of 2000, Pub. L. No. 106-386, 106th Cong., H.R. 3244 (October 28,2000), http://www.gpo.gov/fdsys/pkg/PLAW-106publ386/pdf/PLAW-106publ386.pdf.

[8]In 2000, the UN General Assembly adopted the UN Convention Against Transnational Organized Crime and three accompanying Protocols, including the Palermo Protocol, http://www.uncjin.org/Documents/Conventions/dcatoc/final_documents_2/convention_%20traff_eng.pdf. The Palermo Protocol is an international multilateral treaty and has been ratified by the United States. The United States implements its obligations under the treaty in large part through the Trafficking Victims Protection Act of 2000, as amended.

[9]The Palermo Protocol: available at:
http://www.uncjin.org/Documents/Conventions/dcatoc/final_documents_2/convention_%20traff_eng.pdf;
ILO Convention 182: The Worst Forms of Child Labor: available at:
http://www.ilo.org/public/english/standards/relm/ilc/ilc87/com-chic.htm.

---

million people were trafficked, but only 7,909 traffickers were prosecuted in 2011, of which a mere 3,969 led to convictions.[10] The consequences of low prosecution and conviction rates include the failure to significantly deter the crime of human trafficking and the reluctance among victims to come forth and participate in legal processes that may endanger their safety and produce zero benefit.

***Partnership:*** Successful efforts to combat TIP require effective and efficient coordination across a broad range of stakeholders. Partnerships and coordinating bodies need to focus on bringing together local, national, regional, and global networks, and representatives of civil society, government, the private sector, labor unions, media, universities and faith-based organizations. By increasing coordination, stakeholders are better able to fully leverage a wide range of counter-trafficking interventions. The primary responsibility for C–TIP, however, rests with governments. In the United States, the President's Interagency Task Force to Monitor and Combat Trafficking in Persons brings together federal departments and agencies to ensure a whole-of-government effort that addresses all aspects of human trafficking. In the field, personnel are strongly encouraged to partner with relevant offices at the U.S. Embassy, but also host-government institutions and other donors that address this issue.

Within the Four Ps Paradigm, USAID's C–TIP Policy articulates seven guiding principles that are advanced through five programming objectives.

## Guiding Principles

Employ USAID's Comparative Advantage: USAID's comparative advantage within the U.S. Government and the broader international community derives from in-country expertise, allowing officers to design and monitor well-run interventions informed by local context, and to catalyze other relevant actors. Additionally, to make our investments in TIP more effective, we will move toward a more integrated approach to prevention and protection within our core programs as well as a sharper focus on key segments of the population that are vulnerable to trafficking such as youth and women. We will continue to coordinate and collaborate with our DOS colleagues both in Washington, DC and throughout the world to ensure that duplication of effort is eliminated and that policy and programming interventions are informed by the local environment.

Measure Results and Bring to Scale: USAID is increasing its use of evidence-based interventions in combating trafficking and going forward will employ rigorous methods to measure program effectiveness. The resulting data will be used to scale those activities that empirically demonstrate success and to help establish best practices in prevention and protection within the C–TIP community.

Apply Selectivity and Focus: Through the regular USAID budget process, the Agency will prioritize and increase C–TIP investments in a few select countries. Two types of countries will be favored in this effort: 1) critical TIP challenge countries, e.g. major global players that have long-standing poor TIP rankings according to the DOS annual TIP Report and in which USAID has a Mission and; 2) conflict and post-conflict countries. In these contexts, investments may also be driven by political openings or strategic opportunities to make a major difference along with local partners in C–TIP.

Develop Regional Approaches: TIP is often transnational in nature and therefore requires both national and transnational interventions. To that end, USAID will strengthen regional approaches to most effectively combat cross-border trafficking.

Promote Partnerships: Governments are critical players in combating TIP inside a country, and USAID Missions have a particular role to play helping to grow host-government capacity and galvanize local

---

[10]DOS. 2012. *Trafficking in Persons Report.* Washington, D.C. http://www.state.gov/j/tip/rls/tiprpt/2012/index.htm, 44.

partners. That said, governments alone cannot combat trafficking, and USAID has long relied on close partnerships with the private sector and non-governmental organizations (NGOs) to advance this work.

Invest in Innovation and Technology: Throughout the Agency, USAID is increasingly investing in innovation and technology to meet development challenges with 21st century approaches. We will leverage investments in innovation and technology to combat trafficking.

Promote High Ethical Standards: On September 25, 2012, President Obama released an Executive Order to strengthen protections against TIP in federal contracting.[11] We have also enhanced institutional accountability within USAID to address trafficking through training and coordination. In 2011, USAID adopted a Counter-Trafficking Code of Conduct and implementation guidance that holds Agency employees to the same high ethical standards of behavior with regard to trafficking that federal law requires of contractors and grantees.[12] Additionally, in June 2012, USAID adopted a Counter-Trafficking Standard Operating Procedure that lays out concrete steps for Agency employees to take on the issue of C–TIP.[13]

## Programming Objectives

Integration: USAID will continue direct support to combat trafficking, for example, through work with NGOs providing protection and raising awareness as well as with government institutions, such as parliaments and judiciaries, to strengthen C–TIP capacity. Over time, however, to bring USAID's C–TIP work to a new, more leveraged and robust level, stand-alone projects will have to demonstrate a strong linkage to or be integrated into specific sector portfolios, especially in health, agriculture, economic growth, education, humanitarian assistance, and security sector reform.

Application of Learning: USAID will build rigorous qualitative and, where possible, quantitative approaches that capture the results and impact of C–TIP interventions into new project designs. Specifically, the Agency will support Missions to: (1) increase the use of survey data to guide the design of C–TIP programs; and (2) improve monitoring and evaluation of C–TIP programs.

Augmented C–TIP Investments in Critical TIP Challenge Countries: As part of growing the global movement to combat TIP, USAID will look for opportunities where possible to partner with others in what are called "critical TIP challenge countries"—ones that have global strategic importance and significant trafficking problems; where the host government has done little to prevent or combat TIP; and that have been ranked multiple years as Tier 2 Watch List or Tier 3 in the DOS annual TIP Report. USAID is best placed to do this when there is a Mission presence. These countries provide negative norms and standards on C–TIP in their regions.

Augmented C–TIP Investments in Conflict and Crisis-Affected Areas: As part of USAID's implementation of the 2011 United States National Action Plan on Women, Peace, and Security, USAID will increase its efforts to combat trafficking in a few specific conflict and crisis-affected countries.[14]

---

[11]Executive Order available at: http://www.whitehouse.gov/the-press-office/2012/09/25/executive-order-strengthening-protections-against-trafficking-persons-fe.
[12]Guidance on the Implementation of Agency-Wide Counter Trafficking in Persons Code of Conduct available at: http://pdf.usaid.gov/pdf_docs/PDACT175.pdf.
[13]Counter-Trafficking Standard Operating Procedure available at: http://transition.usaid.gov/policy/C-TIP_SOP.pdf.
[14]National Action Plan available at: http://www.whitehouse.gov/sites/default/files/email-files/US_National_Action_Plan_on_Women_Peace_and_Security.pdf. Executive Order available at: http://www.whitehouse.gov/the-press-office/2011/12/19/executive-order-instituting-national-action-plan-women-peace-and-securit. [sic]

This focus might involve reintegration of child soldiers into society, or on working with the humanitarian assistance community to attend to the special needs of TIP victims, especially vulnerable to TIP in and around conflict and crisis-affected areas.

Enhanced Institutional Accountability: This C–TIP Policy will only be effective if staff are enabled to implement and to personally commit to its realization. Actions to implement USAID's 2011 Code of Conduct on combating TIP include: 1) training staff Agency-wide on combating human trafficking, as well as on the prohibitions on trafficking and procurement of commercial sex, and available disciplinary measures for documented violations; 2) introducing incentives for senior managers to support C–TIP Champions in the field through awards and competitions; 3) educating Agency contractors and recipients on how to recognize and respond to this crime and on the Agency's right to terminate grants and contracts if contractors, grantees, or sub-recipients engage in prohibited conduct; and 4) developing an Agency-wide network of counter-trafficking specialists armed with mechanisms to facilitate communication and information sharing.[15] Collectively, these actions will enable us to proactively combat TIP.

## Implementation

The Center of Excellence on Democracy, Human Rights and Governance (DRG Center) in USAID's Bureau for Democracy, Conflict and Humanitarian Assistance (DCHA) will lead the implementation of the Agency's C–TIP Policy, in collaboration with all USAID Missions and Washington operating units that currently have or plan to program funds to combat TIP.

Mission Directors and staff, in consultation with Regional Bureaus and the DRG Center, will be responsible for program development, management, and related operational issues as part of the normal programming cycle.

DCHA will establish and lead a C–TIP Steering Committee that includes USAID senior leaders and managers in Washington and in the field to coordinate C–TIP programming. The Committee will:

- Oversee the implementation of this Policy.
- Provide technical leadership and support to Missions.
- Lead knowledge collection and management.
- Support planning, strategy, and coordination.
- Oversee (minimal) reporting requirements, ensure alignment and input into existing USAID programming, budgeting and project cycles.
- Assess success and consider solutions to policy and program challenges.

DCHA, in collaboration with the C–TIP Steering Committee, will produce a public document summarizing USAID C–TIP programming. This document, the Annual C–TIP Review, will highlight for external stakeholders the programming that translates this policy into meaningful action for millions of children, women, and men.

---

[15]To build a global movement to combat TIP will involve all of us. In this spirit, to promote creative engagement by a diverse set of colleagues—not just those who are identified as C–TIP Champions—Missions are encouraged to create opportunities to educate and inspire staff to be a part of the movement, such as holding film screenings where relevant films are shown and encouraging colleagues who are not yet directly engaged in the issue on how new and/or existing programs could be additive to a global C–TIP movement.

# PART 2. TRAFFICKING IN PERSONS 101

## Overview of Trafficking in Persons

At its essence, TIP is about people being bought and sold as chattel. Trafficking, or modern slavery, constitutes a violation of human rights in which victims are deprived of their fundamental rights and freedoms. The Quadrennial Diplomacy and Development Review (QDDR), Presidential Policy Directive 6 on Development (2010) (PPD6), and other USG policy instruments explicitly call on USAID to promote moral values, to address the moral dimensions of development, and to elevate human rights. The USAID Policy on C–TIP as well as recently released USAID documents on Gender Equality and Female Empowerment and the establishment of the President's Atrocities Prevention Board have begun to do just that.

The Palermo Protocol defines human trafficking as:

> The recruitment, transportation, transfer, harbouring or receipt of persons, by means of the threat or use of force or other forms of coercion, of abduction, of fraud, of deception, of the abuse of power or of a position of vulnerability or of the giving or receiving of payments or benefits to achieve the consent of a person having control over another person, for the purpose of exploitation. Exploitation shall include, at a minimum, the exploitation of the prostitution of others or other forms of sexual exploitation, forced labour or services, slavery or practices similar to slavery, servitude or the removal of organs.[16]

The Protocol also clarifies that the recruitment, transportation, transfer, harboring, or receipt of an individual under the age of 18 for the purpose of exploitation is considered trafficking in persons, even if none of the means listed above (force, coercion, abduction, etc.) are involved.[17] Therefore, according to the Protocol, minors in prostitution are considered trafficking victims; by definition they cannot have consented to be prostitutes. Although the Protocol focuses on transnational crime, it requires signatory countries to criminalize intentional TIP through national legislation, even in cases where there is no trans-border movement.[18] Trafficking can occur inside a country or even within a single town. Movement, whether transnational or otherwise, while often a component of trafficking, is not a necessary element. The presence of force, fraud, or coercion for the purpose of exploitation is a necessary element of TIP.

---

[16]United Nations General Assembly. 2000. *Protocol to Prevent, Suppress and Punish Trafficking in Persons, Especially Women and Children.* New York, N.Y. http://www.uncjin.org/Documents/Conventions/dcatoc/final_documents_2/convention_%20traff_eng.pdf, Article 3(a).

[17]Ibid., Article 3c-d.

[18]Ibid., Article 5; United Nations. 2000. *United Nations Convention against Transnational Organized Crime.* New York, N.Y., http://www.uncjin.org/Documents/Conventions/dcatoc/final_documents_2/convention_eng.pdf, Article 34 (2); United Nations Office on Drugs and Crime (UNODC). 2004. *Legislative Guides for the Implementation of the United Nations Convention against Transnational Organized Crime and the Protocol Thereto.* New York, N.Y. http://www.unodc.org/pdf/crime/legislative_guides/Legislative%20guides_Full%20version.pdf, 9–11 and 276–77.

---

The TVPA and the Palermo Protocol were both enacted in 2000, and define TIP consistently.[19] Both emphasize the use of force, fraud, or coercion to obtain the services of another person. Both frame the crime of trafficking around the extreme exploitation that characterizes this form of abuse.

On occasion, practitioners mistakenly conflate human trafficking and human smuggling. Article 3 of the UN Protocol against the Smuggling of Migrants by Land, Sea and Air, supplementing the United Nations Convention against Transnational Organized Crime (the "Migrant Smuggling Protocol") defines migrant smuggling as "...the procurement, in order to obtain, directly or indirectly, a financial or other material benefit, of the illegal entry of a person into a State Party of which the person is not a national or a permanent resident."[20]

Article 6 of the Migrant Smuggling Protocol requires the criminalization of this conduct as well as "Enabling a person who is not a national or a permanent resident to remain in the State concerned without complying with the necessary requirements for legally remaining in the State by the means mentioned in subparagraph (b) of this paragraph or any other illegal means."[21]

The distinctions between smuggling and trafficking are often very subtle and the crimes sometimes overlap. The UN Office on Drugs and Crime (UNODC) notes the following technical distinctions between the two crimes:

- Consent - migrant smuggling, while often undertaken in dangerous or degrading conditions, involves consent. Trafficking victims, on the other hand, have either never consented or if they initially consented, that consent has been rendered meaningless by the coercive, deceptive or abusive action of the traffickers.

- Exploitation - migrant smuggling ends with the migrants' arrival at their destination, whereas trafficking involves the ongoing exploitation of the victim.

- Transnationality - smuggling is always transnational, whereas trafficking may not be. Trafficking can occur regardless of whether victims are taken to another state or moved within a state's borders.

- Source of profits - in smuggling cases, profits are derived from the transportation or facilitation of the illegal entry or stay of a person into another county, while in trafficking cases profits are derived from exploitation.[22]

UNODC elaborates on how the two crimes can overlap, or how an initial crime of smuggling can lead to TIP with the following scenarios:

- Some trafficked persons might start their journey by agreeing to be smuggled into a country, but find themselves deceived, coerced or forced into an exploitative situation later in the process (for instance, being forced to work for extraordinary low wages to pay for their transportation).

---

[19]Victims of Trafficking and Violence Protection Act of 2000, Pub. L. No. 106-386, 106th Cong., H.R. 3244 (October 28, 2000),
http://www.gpo.gov/fdsys/pkg/PLAW-106publ386/pdf/PLAW-106publ386.pdf.
[20]UNODC. 2004. *Protocol against the Smuggling of Migrants by Land, Sea and Air.* New York, N.Y.
http://www.unodc.org/documents/treaties/UNTOC/Publications/TOC%20Convention/TOCebook-e.pdf.
[21]This language is taken directly from UNODC. Ibid., Article 6, ¶1(c)
[22]"Migrant Smuggling Frequently Asked Questions," UNODC, accessed January 23, 2013,
http://www.unodc.org/unodc/en/human-trafficking/faqs-migrant-smuggling.html.

---

- Traffickers may present an 'opportunity' that sounds more like smuggling to potential victims. They could be asked to pay a fee in common with other people who are smuggled. However, the intention of the trafficker from the outset is the exploitation of the victim. The 'fee' was part of the fraud and deception and a way to make more money.

- Smuggling may not be the planned intention at the outset but a 'too good to miss' opportunity to traffic people presents itself to the smugglers/traffickers at some point in the process.

- Criminals may both smuggle and traffic people, employing the same routes and methods of transporting them.[23]

## How Does the United States Government Define TIP?

The TVPA does not provide an explicit definition of human trafficking *per se*, but does define "severe forms of trafficking in persons" in the following terms:

- "Sex trafficking in which a commercial sex act is induced by force, fraud, or coercion, or in which the person induced to perform such act has not attained 18 years of age; or

- The recruitment, harboring, transportation, provision, or obtaining of a person for labor or services, through the use of force, fraud, or coercion for the purpose of subjection to involuntary servitude, peonage, debt bondage, or slavery." [24]

The TVPA describes this compelled service using a number of different terms: involuntary servitude, slavery, debt bondage, and forced labor. Under the TVPA, individuals may be trafficking victims regardless of whether they once consented, participated in a crime as a direct result of being trafficked, were transported into the exploitative situation, or were simply born into a state of servitude. At the heart of this phenomenon are the myriad forms of enslavement—whether or not international movement is involved. Under the TVPA, as under the Palermo Protocol, minors in prostitution are *de facto* trafficking victims, regardless of whether they have "consented" to it or not.

According to the TVPA, the term "coercion" refers to threats of serious harm to or physical restraint against any person; any scheme, plan, or pattern intended to cause a person to believe that failure to perform an act would result in serious harm to or physical restraint against any person; or the abuse or threatened abuse of the legal process.

The DOS outlined the following major forms of human trafficking in its 2012 TIP Report.[25] Below we reprint their language.

### Forced Labor

Forced labor, sometimes also referred to as labor trafficking, encompasses the range of activities – recruiting, harboring, transporting, providing, or obtaining – involved when a person uses force or physical threats, psychological coercion, abuse of the legal process, deception, or other coercive means to compel someone to work. Once a person's labor is exploited by such means, the person's previous consent or effort to obtain employment with the trafficker becomes irrelevant. Migrants are particularly vulnerable to this form of human trafficking, but individuals

---

[23]Ibid.
[24]TVPA, Pub. L. No. 106-386, 106th Cong., H.R. 3244 (October 28, 2000), §103(8). http://www.gpo.gov/fdsys/pkg/PLAW-106publ386/pdf/PLAW-106publ386.pdf.
[25]DOS. 2012. *Trafficking in Persons Report (12th Edition)*. Washington, D.C., 33–35.

also may be forced into labor in their own countries. Female victims of forced or bonded labor, especially women and girls in domestic servitude, are often sexually exploited as well.

## Sex Trafficking

When an adult is coerced, forced, or deceived into prostitution – or maintained in prostitution through one of these means after initially consenting – that person is a victim of trafficking. Under such circumstances, perpetrators involved in recruiting, harboring, transporting, providing, or obtaining a person for that purpose are responsible for trafficking crimes. Sex trafficking also may occur within debt bondage, as women and girls are forced to continue in prostitution through the use of unlawful "debt" purportedly incurred through their transportation, recruitment, or even their crude "sale" – which exploiters insist they must pay off before they can be free. A person's initial consent to participate in prostitution is not legally determinative: if one is thereafter held in service through psychological manipulation or physical force, he or she is a trafficking victim and should receive benefits outlined in the Palermo Protocol and applicable domestic laws.

## Bonded Labor or Debt Bondage

One form of coercion is the use of a bond or debt. U.S. law prohibits the use of a debt or other threats of financial harm as a form of coercion and the Palermo Protocol requires its criminalization as a form of trafficking in persons. Some workers inherit debt; for example, in South Asia it is estimated that there are millions of trafficking victims working to pay off their ancestors' debts. Others fall victim to traffickers or recruiters who unlawfully exploit an initial debt assumed as a term of employment. Debt bondage of migrant laborers in their countries of origin, often with the support of labor agencies and employers in the destination country, can also contribute to a situation of debt bondage. Such circumstances may occur in the context of employment-based temporary work programs when a worker's legal status in the country is tied to the employer and workers fear seeking redress.

## Involuntary Domestic Servitude

Involuntary domestic servitude is a form of human trafficking found in unique circumstances—informal work in a private residence—these circumstances create unique vulnerabilities for victims. Domestic workplaces are informal, connected to off-duty living quarters, and often not shared with other workers. Such an environment, which can isolate domestic workers, is conducive to exploitation because authorities cannot inspect homes as easily as they can compared to formal workplaces. Investigators and service providers report many cases of untreated illnesses and, tragically, widespread sexual abuse, which in some cases may be symptoms of a situation of involuntary servitude.

## Forced Child Labor

Although children may legally engage in certain forms of work, forms of slavery or slavery-like practices continue to exist as manifestations of human trafficking, despite legal prohibitions and widespread condemnation. A child can be a victim of human trafficking regardless of the location of that nonconsensual exploitation. Some indicators of possible forced labor of a child include situations in which the child appears to be in the custody of a nonfamily member who requires the child to perform work that financially benefits someone outside the child's family and does not offer the child the option of leaving. Anti-trafficking responses should supplement, not replace, traditional actions against child labor, such as remediation and education. When children are enslaved, however, their abusers should not escape criminal punishment by taking weaker administrative responses to child labor practices.

### Unlawful Recruitment and Use of Child Soldiers

Child soldiering is a manifestation of human trafficking when it involves the unlawful recruitment or use of children – through force, fraud, or coercion – by armed forces as combatants or other forms of labor. Some child soldiers are also sexually exploited by armed groups. Perpetrators may be government armed forces, paramilitary organizations, or rebel groups. Many children are forcibly abducted to be used as combatants. Others are unlawfully made to work as porters, cooks, guards, servants, messengers, or spies. Young girls can be forced to marry or have sex with male combatants. Both male and female child soldiers are often sexually abused and are at high risk of contracting sexually transmitted diseases.

### Child Sex Trafficking

When a child (under 18 years of age) is induced to perform a commercial sex act, proving force, fraud, or coercion against their pimp is not necessary for the offense to be characterized as human trafficking. There are no exceptions to this rule: no cultural or socioeconomic rationalizations should prevent the rescue of children from sexual servitude. The use of children in the commercial sex trade is prohibited both under U.S. law and by statute in most countries around the world. Sex trafficking has devastating consequences for minors, including long-lasting physical and psychological trauma, disease (including HIV/AIDS), drug addiction, unwanted pregnancy, malnutrition, social ostracism, and even death.

## Indicators That a Person May Be a Trafficking Victim

Below are some indicators that a person may be a human trafficking victim. This list is not meant to be exhaustive but rather a point of reference for field practitioners when trying to determine if someone is a TIP victim.

- The person was recruited for one purpose but is working in a different job.

- The person was recruited to work in one country but is working in a different country.

- The person is a minor who is employed but not attending school, particularly if the person exhibits signs of sexual, physical, or psychological abuse or neglect (for example, he or she has bruises/injuries, is malnourished, or appears ill).

- The person is, or appears to have been, forced to perform sexual acts.

- The person is a minor who is selling sex for money.

- The person or his or her family has been threatened with harm if they try to leave the work site or the town or country of the employment opportunity.

- The person is not in possession of his or her identification or travel documents.

- The person's freedom of movement is, or appears to have been, restricted in any way (for example, he or she is working under guard, is prohibited from leaving the work site to go to the bathroom without permission from the employer, or is locked into his or her work site or living quarters at any time).

- The person appears anxious or fearful or exhibits other behaviors that may indicate that he or she has been abused sexually, physically, or psychologically, or that his or her freedom of movement has been restricted.

- The person exhibits signs of physical abuse, such as bruises, black eyes, or other physical injuries.

- The person has been threatened with deportation, law enforcement action, or harm of any kind.

- The person appears to have been drugged or deprived of food, water, sleep, medical care, or other life necessities.

- The person appears to have been deprived of safe and sanitary living conditions.

- The person's wages are withheld by a third party, whether or not in order to pay down a debt.

- The person is incurring a debt to his or her employer during the course of the employment relationship (for example, if the employer is charging the employee for housing/food costs on the work site and these costs exceed or equal the wage the employee is paid).

- The person is unsure of the amount of wages he or she is being paid and uneducated about his or her rights of employment.

- The person lacks freedom of speech (for example, where one official insists on speaking for all workers rather than allowing each worker to respond directly to questions asked by work site visitors or inspectors).

- The person appears to have been coached on what to say to visitors to the work site or to law enforcement.

- The person is prohibited by his or her employer or other persons from freely contacting friends or family.

## What Is NOT Human Trafficking?

As set forth in the 2010 TIP report, the following is not considered TIP: [26]

### Illegal Adoptions

The kidnapping or unlawful buying/selling of an infant or child for the purpose of offering that child for adoption represents a serious criminal offense, but it is not a form of human trafficking, as it does not necessarily involve the use of force, fraud, or coercion to compel services from a person. As stated in the *travaux preparatoires* of the Palermo Protocol, only "where illegal adoption amounts to a practice similar to slavery… it will also fall within the scope of the Protocol."

### The Trade in Human Organs

The trade in human organs—such as kidneys—is not in itself a form of human trafficking. The international trade in organs is substantial and demand appears to be growing. Some victims in developing countries are exploited as their kidneys are purchased for low prices. The Palermo Protocol includes in its definition of illegal human trafficking the recruitment, transportation, transfer, harboring, or receipt of persons by coercive means for the purpose of removal of organs.

---

[26]This language comes from, DOS. 2010. *Trafficking in Persons Report (10th Edition).* Washington, D.C.

## Child Pornography

Sex trafficking of children can involve several different forms of exploitation, including the production of child pornography. However, the production of sexual images representing children—which increasingly includes drawings, the use of mobile phones and computer-generated images—is not sex trafficking unless a child is actually induced to perform a commercial sex act for the purpose of producing the pornography. Distribution and possession of child pornography, while often criminally prohibited, are not acts of human trafficking.[27]

## Prostitution

Prostitution by willing adults is not human trafficking regardless of whether it is legalized, decriminalized, or criminalized. However, pursuant to the Trafficking Victims Protection Reauthorization Act (TVPRA) of 2008, the definitions of human trafficking under U.S. law are not construed to treat prostitution as a legal form of employment.

---

### USAID COUNTERTRAFFICKING IN PERSONS CODE OF CONDUCT: PERSONNEL RESPONSIBILITIES

USAID opposes any activities that may contribute to human trafficking, including the procurement of commercial sex acts and use of forced labor. The Agency therefore prohibits its employees, contractors, subcontractors, grantees, and recipients from engaging in behaviors that facilitate or support TIP. USAID personnel who witness or suspect trafficking are required under the C–TIP Code of Conduct to contact the USAID/OIG at -1-800-230-6539 or 202-712-1023, or via e-mail at ig.hotline@usaid.gov. In addition, personnel in these situations are also encouraged to contact their USAID Regional Legal Advisor within the country.

---

[27]Ninety-four of 187 Interpol member states had laws specifically addressing child pornography as of 2008, though this does not include nations that ban all pornography. Of those 94 countries, 58 criminalized possession of child pornography regardless of intent to distribute. International Center for Missing and Exploited Children. 2008. "Child Pornography, Model Legislation and Global Review." Alexandria, Virginia.

# PART 3. POLICY IMPLEMENTATION BY OBJECTIVE

USAID's C–TIP efforts fully conform to and are complementary of existing USG policies and practices. More specifically, this Counter-Trafficking in Persons Field Guide is intended as a practical resource on how to implement USAID's C–TIP Policy in a wide variety of contexts.

## Integration and Application of Learning Efforts to Combat TIP

USAID will continue direct support to combat trafficking, especially in areas that demand unique focus and attention from the USG, to local government institutions and NGOs in order to tackle truly egregious situations. Over time, however, in order to leverage USAID's C–TIP impact to a robust and sustainable level, stand-alone projects will have to demonstrate a strong linkage to, or be integrated into, specific sector portfolios, especially in health, agriculture, economic growth, education, humanitarian assistance, and security sector reform. Along with our integration efforts and throughout the Agency portfolio, USAID will build into new projects explicit methodologies—when and where possible, quantitative approaches—that capture the impact of the C–TIP interventions. Specifically, the Agency will support Missions to: (1) increase the use of survey data to guide the design of C–TIP programs; and (2) improve monitoring and evaluation of C–TIP programs.

### Integration

The release of the C–TIP Policy provides Missions the unique opportunity to fully integrate C–TIP, where relevant, throughout the entirety of their Country Development and Cooperation Strategy (CDCS) and Program Cycle processes, as well as into additional reporting required throughout the year. This section seeks to walk through those processes with the use of both practical instruction and best practice examples where relevant.

### CDCS

A CDCS is intended to be a collaborative, consultative, results-oriented process that focuses on investments in key areas that shape a country's overall stability and prosperity. Where relevant, this document will also incorporate Agency level priorities and Presidential Initiative strategies, including C–TIP.

The CDCS must contain the following content:

*1.   An Understanding of the Development Context, Challenges and Opportunities*

In order to understand the context, challenges and opportunities inherent in a given country, Missions must engage in a thorough review of country-specific evidence-based literature. During this analytical stage, if Missions find that TIP is a particularly relevant development challenge to be addressed (either due to repeated Tier 2 Watch List or Tier 3 rankings or some other factor), they are encouraged to consult additional literature to help in the formulation of their overall development hypothesis.[28] Additional literature sources can include (but are not limited to)

---

[28]During this stage of analysis, Missions should also think through possible links between TIP, trafficking in weapons and trafficking in narcotics. Not all forms of trafficking will be relevant in all countries in which USAID operates.  In several regions of the world, however, including Central America, the Balkans, and Central Asia, the same routes and sometimes the same networks are used for the trafficking of persons, weapons and narcotics.

- Annual DOS TIP Reports[29]

- Regularly issued ILO research products[30]

- International Organization for Migration (IOM) Research products [31]

- UNICEF State of the World's Children Report and related research products[32]

- Regular UNODC Anti-Trafficking Publications and Tools[33]

- World Bank, Asian Development Bank and International Monetary Fund assessments on the topic.[34]

### 2. A Development Hypothesis

Once the analytical stage of a CDCS is complete and TIP is found to be a relevant issue within the country context, Missions can begin to formulate their development hypothesis. In this stage and dependent on country context, Missions may choose to have C–TIP as part of an overall country-level Development Objective (DO) with supporting Intermediate Results (IRs) and sub-IRs or Missions may find it more appropriate to integrate C–TIP activities at the IR and/or sub-IR level. The decision should be based on thorough analysis of what is relevant in a given country and how that relates to its overall development goals. If Missions need assistance in this effort, they are encouraged to engage both their regional C–TIP Advisors as well as DCHA/DRG.

### 3. Results Framework

The Results Framework is a graphic representation of the development hypothesis that includes the overall DOs as well as IRs, Sub-IRs as well as critical assumptions.

### 4. A Fully Developed Monitoring, Evaluation and Learning Plan

- Missions are required to monitor progress toward achieving or advancing the CDCS Goals, DOs, IRs, and sub-IRs based on the Performance Indicators included in the CDCS. While baseline indicators for C–TIP are limited, a number of resources are available. Examples of performance indicators for TIP activities are listed in Section 1.5.3 of the DOS Guide to Standard Foreign Assistance Indicators.[35] Additionally, this Guide contains sample indicators for consideration by field practitioners. The USAID Europe & Eurasia (E&E) Bureau created an evaluation framework for protection and prevention programs that provides concrete guidance on evaluation for those who are designing and implementing such programs.[36] These Performance Indicators

---

[29]Updated yearly and found at http://www.state.gov/j/tip/.

[30]Found at: http://www.ilo.org/global/publications/lang--en/index.htm.

[31]Updated regularly with both fee for purchase and free products found at: http://publications.iom.int/bookstore/index.php?main_page=index&language=en.

[32]Updated yearly and found at: http://www.unicef.org/sowc2012/.

[33]Updated regularly and found at: http://www.unodc.org/unodc/en/human-trafficking/publications.html.

[34]Found at: http://siteresources.worldbank.org/SOCIALPROTECTION/Resources/SP-Discussion-papers/Labor-Market-DP/0911.pdf; http://aric.adb.org/initiativetable.php?iid=163&ssid=4&title=ADB%20and%20Human%20Trafficking%20in%20Asia.

[35]Found at http://www.state.gov/documents/organization/141836.pdf.

[36]The report is available at http://socialtransitions.kdid.org/library/executive-summary-evaluation-framework-usaid-funded-tip-prevention-and-victim-protection-pro.

will be further developed and refined, along with baselines and targets, in the Mission's Performance Management Plan, developed subsequent to CDCS.

5. *A Fully Developed Understanding of the Program Resources and Priorities as well as Management Requirements Required for the Length of the CDCS*

The CDCS accounts for all projected program resources for fiscal years covered by the period of the CDCS that USAID plans to implement. During this stage in the process, Missions are asked to consider at least two planning scenarios based on a variety of external factors that can include decreased funds availability at the country level; re-prioritization of Agency-level resources; short- and long-term personnel needs and, changing security situations at the implementation level. Furthermore, it is important to note that at this stage of the process, Missions must prioritize among and within DOs. *As of the publication of this Field Guide, TIP has not been identified as a stand-alone DO within the CDCS process, and as such, has not been prioritized on its own within a given country context.*

## Project Design and Implementation

In many instances Missions will have already completed a CDCS or a Transition Strategy. In those cases, personnel should look towards Project Design and Implementation as a mechanism through which to incorporate C–TIP. A project is a set of interventions over an established timeframe and budget that are intended to achieve discrete development results. There are three distinct stages of the Project Design Process: concept, analysis, and approval. What follows is a brief review of each step of that process based on the Agency's Project Design Guidance.[37]

*Concept*

During the concept stage, the basic parameters of the project and its further articulation are established using the CDCS as the departure point. Assuming that C–TIP is fully integrated into the CDCS, many of the steps required in concept development have already been started and in other cases completed (i.e. stakeholder analysis, literature analysis, and strategic partner identification).

Here are the main steps in the concept stage:

Define the Project Team and Problem to be Addressed: Assuming a C–TIP integrated CDCS, the development challenge to be addressed will be largely identified and the appropriate Project Team members fairly self-evident.

Identify and Analyze the Stakeholders and Define Strategic Partners: By the very nature of an integrated project, the pool of stakeholders and strategic partners will be quite diverse. Potential stakeholders in an integrated program could include (but are not limited to):

- Host government representatives such as the Ministry of Justice, Ministry of Education, Ministry of Health, Ministry of Agriculture, Ministry of Labor, Ministry of Internal Affairs, etc.

- Civil society representatives such as those NGOs focusing on labor rights, human rights, advocacy, and gender equality

- Private sector organizations such as those active with corporate social responsibility funds

- Other donors active on the topic

---

[37]USAID. 2011. *Project Design Guidance.* Washington, D.C. http://pdf.usaid.gov/pdf_docs/PDACS686.pdf, December 9.

- Universities

Review Available Knowledge: As discussed above in the CDCS section, this step should include relevant country specific literature (research, evaluations, and lessons learned) on the topic. While potential sources listed above can be broad in nature, at this point, teams should make a concerted effort to collect data on TIP or on the populations believed to be at risk for TIP at the country and/or regional levels. If it has been determined that TIP is a significant concern in the country and little to no micro-level data is available, teams may consider contacting the DCHA C–TIP Team to determine what assistance may be available to help generate data collection. The DCHA C–TIP Team will release a C–TIP survey tool in 2013 to help Missions collect data to inform the design of C–TIP prevention projects and will provide technical assistance to Missions to conduct C–TIP impact assessments. On occasion, DCHA may also be able to co-fund public opinion surveys, assessments, and evaluations with Missions.

Consider Technology-Based Opportunities: Technology (smart phones), social networks and online classified sites are being used by traffickers to market, recruit, sell and exploit for criminal purposes. Many of these efforts are explicit in nature and some are underground.[38] To leverage dynamic partnerships with higher education institutions, the private sector, and NGOs, foster innovation, and employ technology and new media to combat trafficking with a particular focus on prevention and protection USAID launched the "Campus Challenge" in 2012. Just one example of the sort of technology-based opportunities available, the Campus Challenge has two aspects: a technology contest and a research competition. More information can be found at www.challengeslavery.org.

Analysis: Not every project will undergo the same breadth and depth of analysis. USAID does, however, mandate three types of analyses for each project at the concept stage—gender, environmental and sustainability. These analyses are outlined briefly below, and interested personnel are referred to the USAID Automated Directives System (ADS) for further information. Projects designed in highly dynamic environments may, for example, reduce the depth of some aspects of analysis at this stage of design and include them in early stages of project implementation.

- Gender Analysis: All projects must address relevant gender disparities in a manner consistent with the findings of any analytical work performed during development of the Mission's CDCS or project design.[39]

- Environmental Analysis: Drawing upon the previous environmental analysis during strategic planning and the information from the pre-obligation requirement for environmental impact, project design teams must incorporate the environmental recommendations into project planning.[40]

- Sustainability Analysis: This is a new requirement for all project designs. Missions are asked to analyze key sustainability issues and considerations around a host of issues including economic, financial, social soundness, cultural, institutional capacity, political economy, technical/sectoral, and environmental. This analysis also requires a review of the financial costs of the program, its recurrent costs, and its maintenance capability and costs (if applicable), as well as ensuring that future revenues will be adequate. It involves analyzing the institutional capacity that will need to be in place or developed through the project, including systems, policies, and skills. In conflict situations, or other highly volatile environments, sustainability of project benefits may be

---

[38]Mark Latonero. 2011. "Human Trafficking Online: The Role of Social Networking Sites and Online Classifieds." Los Angeles, California: USC Annenberg School for Communication and Journalism, September.
[39]USAID Automated Directives System 201.3.9.3: Gender Analysis.
[40]USAID Automated Directives System 201.3.9.2 (CDCS preparation) and ADS 201.3.11.2.b (environmental impact).

unpredictable. In those cases, this section should describe what benefits may be sustainable and what may be left to future projects to achieve.

Approval: The authorization and approval of any activity that has integrated C–TIP should follow the same process as stand-alone activities as referenced in the USAID Project Design guidance.[41] Those Missions that are engaged in C–TIP activities and which involve direct financial assistance to host governments should adhere to existing ADS guidance on the topic of direct assistance. Furthermore, those Missions engaged in direct assistance agreements with host governments on this topic should coordinate closely with their Embassy and DOS colleagues, as these agreements usually have not only development ramifications, but diplomatic ones as well. Standard good practice for those working in the field on C–TIP should be regular consultations with Embassy colleagues. USAID staff should know their counterparts in the Embassy dealing with C–TIP and other human rights issues and share information and contacts for mutual benefit on a regular basis.

## Additional Reporting

Concurrent to the above referenced CDCS and Program Cycle processes, Missions are required to report throughout the calendar year in documents such as Operational Plans (through Key Issue Narratives), and Performance Plans.

### INTEGRATED APPROACH TO PREVENT RESTAVÈK IN HAITI

FY 2012 funds were granted to NGOs to develop, test and scale up integrated models for preventing and responding to abuse and exploitation that link a range of services provided by USG programs in a limited geographic area. Local networks work closely to provide a full array of services and, by leveraging USG investments in Food and Economic Security, Health and Other Services, and Democracy, Human Rights and Governance, victims and at-risk populations were linked to economic opportunities, education and health services in their communities to achieve greater impact. For example, in selected high-risk communities, the project demonstrated how an integrated approach, including community mobilization and sensitization along with economic strengthening, access to education and other services, prevented dangerous family separation, restavèk, a form of child domestic servitude, or residential care placement, or recruitment of children, youth and women into gangs or sexual exploitation. Projects generated increased social awareness of the risks to women, children and youth, and increased social pressure against sending children, youth and women into potentially harmful situations. They also supported the reintegration of abused, exploited and separated children, youth and women into their family of origin or with relatives in target communities. While limited in geographic scope, these pilot projects made a broader impact by demonstrating effective approaches and advocating for their increased use throughout Haiti. Assistance and encouragement will be provided to the Government of Haiti and to NGOs to include the anti-trafficking law and other needed reforms in human rights law and policies in the next legislative agenda and advocate for their adoption.

Application of Learning: USAID will build into new projects explicit methodologies—and where possible, quantitative approaches—that capture the impact of the C–TIP interventions. Specifically, the Agency will support Missions to: (1) increase the use of survey data to guide the design of C–TIP programs; and (2) improve monitoring and evaluation of C–TIP programs.

As a community, the use of survey data, performance and impact evaluations measuring effectiveness in C–TIP efforts is still in the early stages. That said, USAID's work through MTV End Exploitation and

---

[41]USAID. 2011. *Project Design Guidance.* Washington, D.C. http://pdf.usaid.gov/pdf_docs/PDACS686.pdf, December 9.

Trafficking Foundation (MTV EXIT) in Asia has provided lessons learned in the use of survey data and the conduct of evaluations after a particular C–TIP intervention.[42] USAID, in partnership with the MTV EXIT Foundation, has supported a massive counter-trafficking awareness-raising and prevention campaign in Asia since 2006. To date, the campaign has produced 28 concerts that have reached more than 650,000 young people (with made-for-TV specials reaching tens of millions more), more than 70 television programs and over 6,000 broadcasts of television programming on 13 MTV EXIT channels, and 11 national terrestrial broadcasters reaching 18 Asian countries. The MTV EXIT campaign incorporated an evidence-based approach to designing their intervention by surveying the target population to gauge their level of understanding about trafficking and determine their educational needs. End-line surveys measured the impact of the program's anti-trafficking messaging. Additionally, USAID/Bangladesh and USAID/Nepal will conduct C–TIP High Quality Performance Evaluations in the next calendar year.[43]

Monitoring, Evaluation and Learning (ME&L) Concerns for C–TIP Programming: Those looking to demonstrate the impact and success of USAID programming will need to be aware of some of the broad challenges in the collection of TIP monitoring and evaluation data in order to craft successful projects and informative learning experiences. The majority of numbers currently reported on trafficking are not derived using rigorous research methodology. Trafficking, both the victims and the perpetrators, belong to a sector of society that is difficult to track and even more difficult to quantify. That said, the first step toward collecting relevant data for designing programs and measuring impact is the fielding of benchmark surveys of populations. These surveys can provide population-based estimates of the numbers of people who are trafficked living in a given country. In addition, the data will provide information on knowledge of and attitudes toward trafficking as well as whether services exist for those people who are at a higher risk for re-trafficking. From there, Missions will be able to measure changes in knowledge, attitudes and practice of the demand and supply sides of trafficking and target interventions.

**Prevention:** State of the art prevention efforts begin with benchmark survey data that enable those designing programs to identify their starting point for action. Follow up survey data can then show the levels of awareness achieved. When examining prevention programs, it is also highly recommended that proxy measures are considered. A key consideration for proxy variables should be the level of knowledge imparted by programs and the resulting changes in knowledge, attitudes, and practices among vulnerable populations.

For instance, if the goal of the project is to increase awareness of the dangers and signs of trafficking then the attitudes and awareness of the target population should be initially measured along with a part of the population that will serve as a control group. Or, if the goal is to combat labor trafficking then it may be useful to track the number of people who look for work in areas that could lead them to be trafficked (e.g. women eager to apply for domestic servant positions through newspaper ads).

**Protection:** The successful implementation of protection programs depends upon safely and sustainably identifying and assisting trafficking victims and providing services, such as shelter, security, health, counseling, legal and reintegration assistance, to trafficking survivors. Survivors often struggle with cultural, reintegration, and safety/security issues. Therefore, when conducting evaluations of protection programs, it is critical that the full impact is understood, including unintended consequences. Although evaluation practitioners often try to identify any unintended consequences of programs, it is necessary for protection programs to go one step further. For example, due to social stigmas, some survivors will be ostracized by members of their own community if they are identified as having been trafficked. If those

---

[42] For more information on MTV evaluations, see http://mtvexit.org/wp-content/uploads/2013/02/MTV-EXIT-Impact-Summary-Feb-2013.pdf

[43] Resulting best practices and/or lessons learned from the Bangladesh and Nepal evaluations will be made available through the USAID Development Experience Clearinghouse.

victims are placed in shelters near their home communities, where they risk being identified, the unintended consequence of placing them in the shelter will be social isolation rather than reintegration. Some may even turn to recruiting other trafficking victims. Therefore, it is highly recommended that evaluations of protection projects have at least one research question on unintended consequences. For instance, if a protection project was to establish shelters in Pakistan to assist identified survivors reintegrate, a question posed by the evaluation may be, "What are people's attitudes and actions towards the shelters and those involved? And have these attitudes and actions changed at all during the life of the project?"

**Prosecution:** The majority of USAID C–TIP programs have focused on prevention and protection while other U.S. Government agencies such as the Departments of State and Justice have placed a greater emphasis on prosecution programs. As stated in the C–TIP Policy, to leverage USAID's comparative advantage, the Agency will continue to emphasize prevention and protection in our C–TIP investments. However, to facilitate strong coordination between USAID and other USG partners, USAID staff should be aware of C–TIP law enforcement issues and the impact of prosecution programs being implemented in their regions. The DOS issued its own evaluation policy in February 2012 (http://www.state.gov/s/d/rm/rls/evaluation/2012/184556.htm) and Missions will need to assess whether they need to conduct USAID-specific evaluations, or whether to use evaluations conducted by the DOS.

**Partnerships:** Unfortunately, there is very little literature on how to successfully measure partner program impact. This includes information on how to successfully measure government to government programs. USAID/IDEA is in the process of establishing material for the measurement of partner programs. It is recommended that, in addition to IDEA, those interested in measuring partner programs look at examples by the Millennium Challenge Corporation, which frequently conducts parallel contracting (with multiple partners) and may be able to provide examples of best practices. As a baseline, USAID efforts on C–TIP ought to consider leveraged efforts as one measure: are we bringing new partners to the C–TIP effort and are these partners in turn helping in substantial ways in prevention or protection efforts?

**Conflict/Crisis Zones:** As USAID begins to focus on identifying TIP issues in conflict and crisis-affected zones, it is urgent that the Agency begin to gather evidence on lessons and best practices on implementing successful programs in these areas. A key issue to keep in mind when designing evaluation plans for conflict- and crisis-affected areas is that due to the security challenges in conflict zones, long-term impact evaluations may be difficult to conduct, so other options should also be considered. Maintaining the integrity of the randomized control group can prove challenging if security concerns cause the program to regularly shift the areas where the project is being implemented.

It is important to remember that strong performance evaluations can generate data-based evidence and can be as useful as impact evaluations. In order to craft a strong performance evaluation, program managers will need to work closely with the Mission M&E, or Performance Management, Officer and/or with pertinent DCHA/DRG evaluation specialists.[44]

**Integration:** As has been stated previously, in order to create a robust, far-reaching C–TIP program, Missions should consider integrating C–TIP into current programming sectors. Missions have the option to monitor and evaluate C–TIP either as a cross-cutting theme or as an integrated component of a project.

---

[44]For more information, please refer to "Monitoring, Evaluation and Learning for Fragile States and Peacebuilding Programs" at http://www.socialimpact.com/resource-center/downloads/fragilestates.pdf and "Literature Review: Trafficking in Post-Conflict Situations" at http://transition.usaid.gov/our_work/democracy_and_governance/technical_areas/trafficking/pubs/Trafficking_Conflict_July2006.pdf.

An example of cross-cutting M&E would be if Haiti were to integrate C–TIP activities into a majority of community services. The Mission could then choose to monitor and evaluate the impact of the combined programs on the prevention and protection of survivors and at-risk populations.

USAID's Mission in Senegal is incorporating C–TIP into its education programming, and for example, may consider having C–TIP be an integrated part of its evaluation of the education program. In this instance, one of the questions that the evaluation would investigate would be, "How has the education system prevented children from being trafficked?" Additionally, those Missions that are just beginning to integrate TIP could use evaluations to see whether or not TIP was successfully integrated, using such evaluation questions as, "How well was TIP integrated into the education program and how could it be improved?"

## Augmented C–TIP Investments in Critical TIP Challenge Countries

USAID is defining critical TIP challenge countries as ones that have global strategic importance and significant trafficking problems; where the host government has done little to prevent or combat TIP; that have been ranked multiple years as Tier 2 Watch List or Tier 3 in the DOS annual TIP Report and where USAID Mission presence exists. These countries set negative norms and standards on C–TIP in their regions. These countries also serve to illustrate the importance of approaching C–TIP from both an internal (within a country's borders) and external (regional) context. The problem of TIP does not follow neatly along bureaucratic lines and in order to effectively tackle the issue, a neighborhood of countries that are affected must come together.

To help leverage our comparative advantage, USAID will increase its dedicated C–TIP resources in one to two critical TIP challenge countries with a USAID Mission presence. Progress in these nations would send an important signal with potentially significant ripple effects. Additionally, a focus in these countries would allow the greatest harmonization of U.S. diplomatic and development efforts. To move a country from one tier to another requires indigenous political will and resources currently beyond what, for example, USAID alone is able to commit. By increasing the focus on one or two of these challenge countries, however, USAID's approach will be to engage and leverage additional partners to elevate solutions to these longstanding TIP obstacles.

## Increased C–TIP Investments in Conflict and Crisis-Affected Areas

As part of USAID's implementation of the 2011 United States National Action Plan on Women, Peace, and Security, USAID will increase its efforts to combat trafficking in a few specific conflict and crisis-affected countries. The criteria for selecting these countries, both through the National Action Plan and the C–TIP Policy, include but are not limited to: significant USG investment; multiyear international deployments with a significant number (such as over 10,000) of personnel deployed; and opportunities to build partnerships with other donors or stakeholders. In addition to new Agency-wide training on ethical standards related to the C–TIP Code of Conduct, USAID will provide training and technical assistance to personnel in selected Missions to design, implement, monitor, and evaluate effective C–TIP interventions in conflict-affected areas. USAID, led by C–TIP Champions and RLAs housed in Missions in conflict and crisis-affected areas, will educate civilian contractors and aid workers on the prevention of TIP in crisis and conflict-affected environments. In some Missions, this effort may include targeted knowledge assessments and social marketing campaigns. Personnel need to be familiar with the 2012 Standard Operating Procedure and the Executive Order on increasing contractor compliance with C–TIP. [45]

---

[45] Executive Order available at: http://www.whitehouse.gov/the-press-office/2012/09/25/executive-order-strengthening-protections-against-trafficking-persons-fe. Guidance on the Implementation of Agency-Wide Counter-Trafficking in Persons Code of Conduct available at: http://pdf.usaid.gov/pdf_docs/PDACT175.pdf.

In conflict and post-conflict areas, displaced and endangered people make desperate decisions, including relying on smugglers (who may turn out to be traffickers) in an attempt to get out of harm's way. In recent years, we have seen examples of women fleeing the conflict in Kosovo and children from the refugee camps in East and West Timor being victimized by traffickers, and, increasingly, of Colombians victimized in the trafficking "market." There is also a problem of international military/peace keeping presence contributing to the growth of trafficking in some areas.[46] The influx of cash associated with a large UN or other international presence can warp local economies and social norms, and effect the demand for prostitution and other illicit activities/practices that were less or uncommon before the conflict.

## EMBEDDED

In many instances, USAID direct-hire personnel or implementers are embedded with US, international and host-government military personnel and/or security contractors in order to advance civilian development objectives. More often than not, these colleagues are serving with great honor and distinction. However, there are documented cases when military and/or security contractors have engaged in trafficking and the exploitation of local populations and third country nationals. In those instances, USAID personnel who witness or suspect trafficking are required under the C–TIP Code of Conduct to contact that USAID/OIG at 1-800-230-6539 or 202-712-1023, or via e-mail at ig.hotline@usaid.gov. In addition, personnel in these situations are also encouraged to contact their USAID Regional Legal Advisor within the country.

In conflict and crisis affected areas, as in other regions, the manner in which men and women are impacted by the conflict is different. That difference should be explored as Missions and host country governments create mechanisms to counter trafficking. In post-conflict contexts male members of a society are often disproportionately recruited in armed conflicts or killed. Under these circumstances, women and children are disproportionately represented among internally displaced and refugee populations. As their socioeconomic support network is diminished, and there are significant delays in their reintegration or resettlement, women and children become even more vulnerable to criminal actors. In other countries, such as Afghanistan and Pakistan, a nexus between human trafficking, human smuggling and social mores regarding the treatment of young boys and girls and the use of forced and/or bonded labor is evident.

During periods of conflict or following conflict in a country, overall lawlessness or diminished rule of law often occur. Until basic infrastructure and legal order is established or reestablished, crime and violence tend to increase and the most vulnerable members of society are victimized. It is in these social circumstances that TIP thrives, with very little threat of law enforcement taking action against the offenders. At their core, conflict and post-conflict societies struggle with poverty, a difficult socioeconomic environment, and lack of employment opportunities—or, in times of conflict, lack of employment opportunities outside of the armed conflict. Economic insecurity and poverty that may have existed prior to the conflict are further aggravated by the political instability that often comes with conflict or post-conflict situations. With a lack of economic opportunities, individuals become more vulnerable to trafficking situations.

---

[46]Corinna Csaky, *No One to Turn To: The Underreporting of Child Sexual Exploitation and Abuse by Aid Workers and Peacekeepers,* (London, England: Save the Children UK, 2008),http://www.savethechildren.org.uk/resources/online-library/no-one-to-turn-to-the-under-reporting-of-child-sexual-exploitation-and-abuse-by-aid-workers-and-peacekeepers; and Sarah E. Mendelson, *Barracks and Brothels: Peace Keepers and Human Trafficking* (Washington, D.C.: Center for Strategic and International Studies, 2005), http://csis.org/files/media/csis/pubs/0502_barracksbrothels.pdf.

Additionally, conflicts inevitably lead to situations where orphaned children or children left with only one parent are forced to support their households, making them especially vulnerable to trafficking or dangerous labor situations. Children, particularly those who have been orphaned, displaced, or separated from family members, are vulnerable to being forcibly recruited for combat, for other forms of forced labor, or as sex slaves by armed groups. In addition, children who have been directly involved in conflicts may have a difficult time readjusting to civil life and may thus become vulnerable to trafficking situations. The lack of a functioning school system in a conflict or post-conflict country is also a factor propagating trafficking in children.

Due to the multi-faceted nature of trafficking, but particularly in conflict and crisis affected states, it is imperative for Missions to envision interventions from all strategic and operational perspectives internal to USAID but also within the whole of USG context; in many instances, Missions will be working directly with the U.S. and international military forces. Those countries which present both a development and security challenge in fact do require some degree of integrated civilian-military planning to tackle not only security issues, but also a set of cross-cutting issues that impact security. These issues may include the movement of people within a given country and across international borders. Further, this examination will also take into account questions surrounding porous national borders and direct impacts on U.S. interests from a more strategic level that is beyond the scope of this Field Guide.

As Missions prepare their planning documents (e.g. CDCS, Transition Strategy, Program Cycle), it is advised that during the analytical stage they not only review literature but also fully engage with donor, civilian and military counterparts in order to ensure that a full picture of potential trafficking problems are known. This engagement will help ensure that a solution may be proposed and implemented which leverages USAID's expertise when and where appropriate.

Those consultations with on-the-ground practitioners should provide a clearer picture of what types of trafficking may be happening in a given context. For example, Missions may be dealing with issues such as unaccompanied children, children and adults in forced labor, third country nationals trafficked to provide services in and around military installations and prostitution. Each of these examples requires a very targeted response. In other words, there is no "one size fits all" solution to counter this problem. Once full consultation with relevant stakeholders has taken place, Missions should be able to determine what type of intervention is most appropriate in a given context. This may include a solely development-focused intervention that provides an integrated package of services to victims, capacity development services for a host government on the topic of trafficking or, a program that is complementary to existing interventions conducted by other USG actors.

In the concept stage, while Missions are planning a specific intervention, staff should assess the budget and resource implications for such an intervention. In conflict- and crisis-affected areas programmatic budgets and personnel resources are consistently subject to change due to issues that are simply outside daily control. In light of this fact, Missions should plan alternatives—more than one budget and resource scenario—in order to ensure that programs are able to endure, at a minimum, for the time-frame originally envisioned.

Finally, in these environments, the ability to regularly monitor and evaluate program implementation is constrained due to factors mentioned above. Consistent with the USAID Evaluation Policy, Missions need to formulate their M&E plans at the concept stage, with the understanding that those plans may have to shift with changes in the political, economic, or security situation. When regular access to program sites is not possible, Missions have the following M&E options:

- Use of Local Personnel and/or Organizations

  ➤ This could be through the use of existing Foreign Service National Personnel or locally engaged M&E Organizations.

- Engagement of a Third Party, Independent M&E Firm

  ➤ Many Missions with large portfolios, or an emphasis on ME&L, have contracted independent, third party M&E specialists for the entire Mission. Others may need to contract out on an as-needed basis or use the IQC mechanisms established with DCHA/DRG or PPL. Additional information on these mechanisms is available through the Mission M&E Specialist.

- Satellite and other Technologies

  ➤ USAID's Geospatial Information web-page is a resource: http://inside.usaid.gov/EGAT/gis/.

## Enhanced Institutional Accountability

The USAID C–TIP Policy will only be effective if staff are enabled to implement and to personally commit to its realization. On National Freedom Day, February 1, 2011, USAID adopted an Agency-wide C–TIP Code of Conduct. This Code of Conduct holds all USAID personnel to the same high ethical standards of behavior with regard to trafficking that federal law requires of USG contractors and recipients. The Code prohibits employees, contractors, subcontractors, grantees, and recipients from engaging in any behavior that may facilitate trafficking, including procuring commercial sex. Under the Code, USAID employees are obligated to report any suspected trafficking activity involving employees, contractors, subcontractors, grantees, and recipients to USAID's Office of Inspector General (the OIG.)[47] The Agency also pledges under the Code to educate personnel about trafficking. To implement the Code, the Agency has taken the following actions:

- *New Civil Service Employees Orientation:* All Civil Service employees new to USAID will receive C–TIP training through the mandatory New Employee Orientation. The C–TIP session focuses on the definition of TIP, the various forms of TIP, and employee obligations under the C–TIP Code of Conduct.

- *New Foreign Service Officers Orientation:* All new career competitive Foreign Service officers will receive C–TIP training through the Development Leadership Initiative. Additionally, all new

---

[47]Please note that the Code of Conduct should not in any way hinder USAID programs that interact directly with sex workers, for example those that conduct HIV/AIDS prevention programs to most at-risk populations (MARPs).

Foreign Service Limited officers deploying to Afghanistan will receive C–TIP training through the Afghanistan Pre-Departure Training. This C–TIP session also focuses on the definition of TIP, the various forms of TIP, and employee obligations under the C–TIP Code of Conduct.

- *Ethics Training for all USAID Employees:* C–TIP is incorporated into the annual ethics refresher course, which is mandatory for all USAID employees, both in Washington, D.C. and in the field.

- *OIG Investigations Personnel:* While USAID itself does not conduct training for OIG investigators, the investigators regularly receive training and periodic updates from the Department of Justice (DOJ) on a variety of issues, including C–TIP. Additionally, USAID/DCHA and OIG collaborate closely on TIP-related issues. USAID/DCHA has distributed a C–TIP information packet to all OIG investigations personnel to provide further guidance on investigating TIP in government contracts and assistance awards.

> The Code prohibits personnel, contractors and grantees from engaging in any behaviors that may facilitate trafficking, including procuring commercial sex. Under the Code, USAID employees are obligated to report suspected trafficking activity to USAID's Office of Inspector General.

- *Contracting Officers (COs), Agreement Officers (AOs), Contracting Officer Representatives (CORs) and Agreement Officer Representatives (AORs):* C–TIP training is available to all acquisition personnel through the Federal Acquisition Institute (FAI). FAI offers an in-depth online training module specifically developed for acquisition personnel, which provides an overview of TIP, a summary of relevant laws and regulations, and a detailed explanation of the roles and responsibilities of different acquisition personnel.

## *C–TIP Clause in Every Contract, Grant and Cooperative Agreement*

Consistent with the TVPA, the Federal Acquisitions Regulation (FAR) requires that clause 52.222-50, Combating Trafficking in Persons, is included in all solicitations and contracts.[48] When procuring commercial items, C–TIP requirements are incorporated through paragraph (a) of FAR 52.212-5, Contract Terms and Conditions Required to Implement Statutes or Executive Orders—Commercial Items.

In addition, all assistance awards to U.S. and Non-U.S. non-governmental recipients must include the Mandatory Standard Provision entitled "Trafficking in Persons." [49]

All mandatory clauses/provisions prohibiting TIP are included in the Global Acquisition and Assistance System, which Agency contracting officers and agreement officers are required to use to generate all Agency awards.

All future audits conducted by the OIG will verify compliance with these federal and agency-specific requirements.

## *Internal Guidance*

USAID's Procurement Executive issued a Procurement Executive Bulletin (PEB) in December 2012 that applies to all COs and AOs and Acquisition and Assistance staff worldwide. The purpose of *PEB 2012-07 Trafficking in Persons* is to remind COs and AOs of their responsibilities for implementing the

---

[48]48 C.F.R. 52.222-50, Combating Trafficking in Persons. See Annex A for mandatory C–TIP language for contracts.

[49]ADS 303. See Annex A for mandatory C–TIP language for Agreements.

requirements of the several federal TIP statutes and to provide additional guidance for more effective compliance.[50]

## Past Performance

The FAR requires that contractor performance information be collected (FAR Part 42) and used in source selection evaluations (FAR Part 15).

Past Performance evaluations provide essential information to make better acquisition decisions and significant incentives to contractors to provide superior supplies and services. Contractors' compliance with and implementation of TIP requirements will be reflected in their past performance evaluations in the Performance Assessment Reporting Systems (CPARS).

---

[50]The PEB is posted at: http://inside.usaid.gov/M/OAA/policy/PEBs/docs/PEB2012_07.doc).

# ANNEX A. STANDARD LANGUAGE FOR CONTRACTS AND COOPERATIVE AGREEMENTS

## Standard C-TIP Language for Contracts

Pursuant to FAR section 22.1705(a) the following basic clause should be inserted in all solicitations and contracts: Combating Trafficking in Persons

(a) Definitions. As used in this clause—

"Coercion" means—

(1) Threats of serious harm to or physical restraint against any person;

(2) Any scheme, plan, or pattern intended to cause a person to believe that failure to perform an act would result in serious harm to or physical restraint against any person; or

(3) The abuse or threatened abuse of the legal process.

"Commercial sex act" means any sex act on account of which anything of value is given to or received by any person.

"Debt bondage" means the status or condition of a debtor arising from a pledge by the debtor of his or her personal services or of those of a person under his or her control as a security for debt, if the value of those services as reasonably assessed is not applied toward the liquidation of the debt or the length and nature of those services are not respectively limited and defined.

"Employee" means an employee of the Contractor directly engaged in the performance of work under the contract who has other than a minimal impact or involvement in contract performance.

"Forced Labor" means knowingly providing or obtaining the labor or services of a person—

(1) By threats of serious harm to, or physical restraint against, that person or another person;

(2) By means of any scheme, plan, or pattern intended to cause the person to believe that, if the person did not perform such labor or services, that person or another person would suffer serious harm or physical restraint; or

(3) By means of the abuse or threatened abuse of law or the legal process.

"Involuntary servitude" includes a condition of servitude induced by means of—

(1) Any scheme, plan, or pattern intended to cause a person to believe that, if the person did not enter into or continue in such conditions, that person or another person would suffer serious harm or physical restraint; or

(2) The abuse or threatened abuse of the legal process.

"Severe forms of trafficking in persons" means—

(1) Sex trafficking in which a commercial sex act is induced by force, fraud, or coercion, or in which the person induced to perform such act has not attained 18 years of age; or

(2) The recruitment, harboring, transportation, provision, or obtaining of a person for labor or service through the use of force, fraud, or coercion for the purpose of subjection to involuntary servitude, peonage, debt bondage, or slavery;

"Sex trafficking" means the recruitment, harboring, transportation, provision, or obtaining of a person for the purpose of a commercial sex act.

b) Policy. The United States Government has adopted a zero tolerance policy regarding trafficking in persons. Contractors and contractor employees shall not—

(1) Engage in severe forms of trafficking in persons during the period of performance of the contract;

(2) Procure commercial sex acts during the period of performance of the contract; or

(3) Use forced labor in the performance of the contract.

(c) Contractor requirements. The Contractor shall—

(1) Notify its employees of—

(i) The United States Government's zero tolerance policy described in paragraph (b) of this clause; and

(ii) The actions that will be taken against employees for violations of this policy. Such actions may include, but are not limited to, removal from the contract, reduction in benefits, or termination of employment; and

(2) Take appropriate action, up to and including termination, against employees or subcontractors that violate the policy in paragraph (b) of this clause.

(d) Notification. The Contractor shall inform the Contracting Officer immediately of—

(1) Any information it receives from any source (including host country law enforcement) that alleges a Contractor employee, subcontractor, or subcontractor employee has engaged in conduct that violates this policy; and

(2) Any actions taken against Contractor employees, subcontractors, or subcontractor employees pursuant to this clause.

(e) Remedies. In addition to other remedies available to the Government, the Contractor's failure to comply with the requirements of paragraphs (c), (d), or (f) of this clause may result in—

(1) Requiring the Contractor to remove a Contractor employee or employees from the performance of the contract;

(2) Requiring the Contractor to terminate a subcontract;

(3) Suspension of contract payments;

(4) Loss of award fee, consistent with the award fee plan, for the performance period in which the Government determined Contractor non-compliance;

(5) Termination of the contract for default or cause, in accordance with the termination clause of this contract; or

(6) Suspension or debarment.

(f) Subcontracts. The Contractor shall include the substance of this clause, including this paragraph (f), in all subcontracts.

(g) Mitigating Factor. The Contracting Officer may consider whether the Contractor had a Trafficking in Persons awareness program at the time of the violation as a mitigating factor when determining remedies. Additional information about Trafficking in Persons and examples of awareness programs can be found at the website for the Department of State's Office to Monitor and Combat Trafficking in Persons at http://www.state.gov/j/tip.

(End of clause)

## Alternative C–TIP Language for Contracts With Specific Directives

Pursuant to FAR Section 22.1705(b), the basic clause (above) is modified when the contract will be performed outside the United States (as defined in FAR Section 25.003) and where "the contracting officer has been notified of specific U.S. directives or notices regarding combating trafficking in persons (such as general orders or military listings of 'off-limits' local establishments) that apply to contractor employees at the contract place of performance."[51]

In this case, the CO should substitute the following paragraph in place of paragraph (c)(1)(i) of the basic clause:

> (i)(A) The United States Government's zero tolerance policy described in paragraph (b) of this clause; and

> (B) The following directive(s) or notice(s) applicable to employees performing work at the contract place(s) of performance as indicated below:

> [Contracting Officer shall insert title of directive/notice; indicate the document is attached or provide source (such as website link) for obtaining document; and, indicate the contract performance location outside the U.S. to which the document applies.]

## Standard C–TIP Language for Cooperative Agreements

Grants and Cooperative Agreements must include the following mandatory clause, pursuant to ADS 303:

TRAFFICKING IN PERSONS (JUNE 2012)

a. USAID is authorized to terminate this award, without penalty, if the recipient or its employees, or any subrecipient or its employees, engage in any of the following conduct:

(1) Trafficking in persons (as defined in the Protocol to Prevent, Suppress, and Punish Trafficking in Persons, especially Women and Children, supplementing the UN Convention against Transnational Organized Crime) during the period of this award;

(2) Procurement of a commercial sex act during the period of this award; or

(3) Use of forced labor in the performance of this award.

b. For purposes of this provision, "employee" means an individual who is engaged in the performance of this award as a direct employee, consultant, or volunteer of the recipient or any subrecipient.

---

[51] 48 CFR 22.1705(b).

c. The recipient must include in all subagreements, including subawards and contracts, a provision prohibiting the conduct described in a(1)-(3) by the subrecipient, contractor or any of their employees.

[END OF PROVISION]

In addition to the above referenced standard provisions for contracts and agreements, some Missions have chosen to develop tailored language on the topic of C–TIP to fit their individual country contexts. What follows below is one such example from Ghana.

## COUNTRY SPECIFIC LANGUAGE: GHANA FEED THE FUTURE

The US Government is committed to the elimination of the worst forms of child labor internationally. As part of these efforts, the [Participant/Contractor/Grantee] shall address—in an appropriate and mutually agreed upon manner with USAID—child labor concerns including any work which, by its nature or the circumstances in which it is carried out, is likely to harm the health, safety or morals of children and any work which is likely to interfere with a child's education. For the purpose of this agreement a child is defined as a person less than 18 years of age. The [Participant/Contractor/Grantee] shall use as a guide relevant international standards on the elimination of child labor including International Labor Organization Convention 182 on the Worst Forms of Child Labor, Convention 138 on the Minimum Age for Work, and the Protocol to Prevent, Suppress, and Punish Trafficking in Persons, Especially Women and Children, all of which have been ratified by the Government of Ghana. All activities designed by the [Participant/Contractor/Grantee] to address child labor concerns must align with the Government of Ghana's laws, policies and priorities regarding child labor including the Children's Act, hazardous work lists, the National Plan of Action (NPA) on the Elimination of the Worst Forms of Child Labor (2008-2015), and Ghana's Human Trafficking Act.

The Government of Ghana has prioritized nine worst forms of child labor including fishing and agriculture. The Feed the Future Initiative is focused on the agriculture sector (rice, maize and soya) in Northern Ghana, increased resiliency of vulnerable households in the Northern Region and fishing sector in the Western Coastal region.

USAID [Agreements/Contracts] funded under the Feed the Future Initiative in Ghana must design and implement strategies to ensure that the efforts to increase productivity, expand trade and markets, and increase resiliency of vulnerable households properly address child labor concerns where relevant. Such efforts may include for example, training, capacity building and awareness raising activities among farmers, communities and children on the worst forms of child labor and work place hazards and safety standards; establishment of community monitoring systems in cooperation with the Government of Ghana Child Labor Monitoring Systems (GCLMS); and research and policy analysis aimed at improving the knowledge base on child labor. USAID expects that all efforts carried out under the Feed the he Future Initiative will be designed to coordinate and complement the Governments efforts. Proposed activities are also expected to complement and not duplicate efforts being carried out by other USG agencies or those carried by bi-lateral or multilateral donors, International Organizations, NGOs, workers' organizations, employer's organizations or other civil society organizations.

# ANNEX B. ROLES AND RESPONSIBILITIES OF USG ENTITIES IN COMBATING HUMAN TRAFFICKING

(All information in Annex B is cited directly from the DOS Office to Monitor and Combat Trafficking in Persons website.)

## The President's Interagency Task Force

The President's Interagency Task Force to Monitor and Combat Trafficking (PITF) is a Cabinet-level entity created by the Trafficking Victims Protection Act of 2000 (TVPA) to coordinate federal efforts to combat trafficking in persons. The PITF meets annually and is chaired by the Secretary of State. The Obama Administration's third annual meeting of the President's Interagency Task Force to Monitor and Combat Trafficking in Persons (PITF) was held on March 15, 2012. At the meeting, leaders from across the Administration highlighted recent accomplishments and the U.S. government's priorities for combating modern slavery in the coming year. Participants included then-Secretary of State Clinton, Attorney General Eric Holder, Secretaries Hilda Solis, Kathleen Sebelius, and Janet Napolitano, Assistant to the President for National Security Affairs, Thomas E. Donilon, Senior Advisor to the President and Chair of the White House Council on Women and Girls, Valerie Jarrett, and Director of the Domestic Policy Council, Cecilia Muñoz, among many other agency leaders. [52]

## Senior Policy Operating Group

The TVPA as amended in 2003 also established the Senior Policy Operating Group (SPOG), which consists of senior officials designated as representatives of the PITF members. The SPOG coordinates interagency policy, grants, research, and planning issues involving international trafficking in persons and the implementation of the TVPA. The SPOG meets quarterly and is chaired by Ambassador-at-Large Luis CdeBaca who also leads the Office to Monitor and Combat Trafficking in Persons at the U.S. Department of State.[53]

## Principal Roles of USG Agencies

The following section is cited directly from the DOS Office to Monitor and Combat Trafficking in Persons.

**Department of State** (DOS): DOS represents the United States in the global fight to combat human trafficking by engaging with foreign governments, international and inter-governmental organizations, and civil society to develop and implement effective strategies for confronting this form of modern slavery. This occurs through bilateral and multilateral diplomacy, targeted foreign assistance, public outreach, and specific projects on trafficking in persons. The Department chairs the PITF and SPOG, as described above. The **Office to Monitor and Combat Trafficking in Persons** produces the annual *Trafficking in Persons Report*, which assesses the strengths and weaknesses of foreign governments' efforts to address human trafficking and serves as the U.S. government's principal diplomatic tool to promote anti-trafficking reforms. The Report also spotlights the forms that modern slavery takes around the world and encourages partnerships with civil society. The office also funds

---

[52]See http://www.state.gov/j/tip/response/usg/index.htm.

[53]Ibid.

---

COUNTER-TRAFFICKING IN PERSONS FIELD GUIDE

international anti-trafficking programs, taking into account the assessments of individual countries as set out in the annual TIP Report. The **Bureau of Population, Refugees, and Migration (PRM)** funds international anti-trafficking programs, as well as the **Return, Reintegration, and Family Reunification Program for Victims of Trafficking**. In addition, global programs funded by the **Bureau of Democracy, Human Rights, and Labor** (DRL) promote worker rights and address labor violations, including trafficking in persons. The Department's security and law enforcement arm, the **Bureau of Diplomatic Security**, plays an essential role investigating human trafficking crimes in collaboration with other law enforcement entities. The **Office of Global Women's Issues** (S/GWI) works for the political, economic, and social empowerment of women. Integral to this work is a focus on responding to and preventing violence against women, which contributes to efforts to prevent human trafficking. The Department's consular officers also have an important role and are trained in combating trafficking in persons at U.S. embassies and consulates worldwide, in particular in issuing employment- or education-based nonimmigrant visas.[54]

**Department of Defense** (DoD): DoD endeavors to ensure that the U.S. military, its civilian employees, and its contractors are aware of and adopt the zero tolerance policy on human trafficking. A demand reduction campaign helps make contractors, government personnel, and military members aware of common signs of human trafficking and provides a hotline number to report suspected incidents. The awareness campaign is reinforced by the requirement for all military and civilian members of the Department to take annual trafficking awareness training. DoD's subordinate organizations are further required to report on completion of their personnel's annual training. Public service announcements on labor and sex trafficking are in effect. DoD routinely holds conferences and workshops to further educate personnel and explore innovative measures to combat TIP.

**Department of Justice** (DOJ): The Human Trafficking Prosecution Unit, a specialized anti-trafficking unit of DOJ's Civil Rights Division's Criminal Section, prosecutes traffickers in partnership with U.S. Attorneys' Offices nationwide. The cases are investigated by the Federal Bureau of Investigation or the Department of Homeland Security's Immigration and Customs Enforcement as well as other federal, state, and local law enforcement agencies. Its national complaint line is 1-888-428-7581. The Criminal Division's Child Exploitation and Obscenity Section prosecutes cases of child sex trafficking and child sex tourism. The Criminal Division's Overseas Prosecutorial Development, Assistance and Training program (OPDAT) provides anti-trafficking training and technical assistance to prosecutors internationally. The International Criminal Investigative Training Assistance Program (ICITAP) works with host country law enforcement agencies to improve their institutional functioning and their ability to interact effectively with other government service providers and with civil society organizations to prevent TIP, protect victims, and prosecute TIP crimes. The Bureau of Justice Assistance funds 38 anti-trafficking task forces comprised of local, state, and federal law enforcement as well as nongovernmental victim service providers. The Office of Victims of Crime funds nongovernmental organizations to provide services to U.S. citizen victims and foreign victims prior to certification by the Department of Health and Human Services. Significant research is conducted by the National Institute of Justice and the Bureau of Justice Statistics. DOJ also produces the Attorney General's Annual Report to Congress on U.S. Government Activities to Combat Trafficking in Persons.

**Department of Agriculture** (USDA): The USDA established a Consultative Group to Eliminate the Use of Child Labor and Forced Labor in Imported Agricultural Products, pursuant to Section 3205 of the Food, Conservation, and Energy Act of 2008. The group represents a diverse set of government, private sector, academic, and nongovernmental organization entities, and has been charged with developing and making recommendations to the Secretary of Agriculture regarding guidelines to reduce the likelihood

---

[54]The following section is cited directly from the DOS Office to Monitor and Combat Trafficking in Persons. See http://www.state.gov/j/tip/response/usg/agencies/index.htm.

that agricultural products imported into the United States are produced with the use of child or forced labor. Within one year after receiving these recommendations, the Secretary is required to finalize the guidelines and release them for public comment.

**Department of Labor** (DOL): DOL's Wage and Hour Division (WHD) carries out civil law enforcement in the nation's workplaces and its field investigators are often the first government authorities to detect exploitive labor practices. WHD coordinates with other law enforcement agencies to ensure restitution on behalf of victims of trafficking. To enhance this coordination, WHD is part of the Anti-Human Trafficking Coordination Team (ACTeam) pilot program that is being developed by the Federal Enforcement Working Group on trafficking (headed by the Department of Justice). WHD has responsibility for certifying U-Visas per the TVPA and has established protocols for certification based on five qualifying criminal activities – involuntary servitude, peonage, trafficking, obstruction of justice and witness tampering – when it detects them in the process of investigating a violation of an employment law under its jurisdiction, such as minimum wage or overtime. DOL's **Employment and Training Administration** offers job search, placement and counseling services, and vocational skills training to trafficking victims. Additionally, DOL's **Bureau of International Labor Affairs** (ILAB) awards grants to implement programs to combat exploitive child labor around the globe. Many of these programs have direct service, awareness raising, and policy activities to address child trafficking as one of the worst forms of child labor. ILAB publishes three reports on child labor and/or forced labor in countries worldwide, including the "List of Goods Produced by Child or Forced Labor" required by the Trafficking Victims Protection Reauthorization Act of 2005 (TVPRA list), which informs the public about 128 goods from 70 countries that DOL has reason to believe are produced by forced labor, child labor, or both in violation of international standards. DOL uses the TVPRA list and other reports as tools to communicate the urgent need for effective action by governments, private sector actors, and others to address these problems.

**Department of Health and Human Services** (HHS): HHS leads the Rescue & Restore Victims of Human Trafficking public awareness campaign, funds organizations to conduct outreach to foreign and U.S. citizen victims, funds comprehensive case management and support services for foreign victims in the United States, and certifies foreign victims of a severe form of trafficking in persons to be eligible to receive Federal benefits and services to the same extent as refugees. A range of programs also assist youth at-risk of trafficking, including the Runaway and Homeless Youth Program. HHS also funds the National Human Trafficking Resource Center that provides a nationwide 24/7 hotline at 1-888-373-7888.

**Department of Education** (ED): ED's Office of Safe and Healthy Students in the Office of Elementary and Secondary Education uses the Web, listservs, and trainings to raise awareness both to prevent trafficking of children and to increase victim identification of trafficked children in schools. Trafficking often involves school-age children—particularly those not living with their parents—who are vulnerable to coerced labor abuse, domestic servitude, and commercial sexual exploitation. Traffickers target minor victims through social networking sites, on the street, in malls, as well as by using students to recruit other students at school and in after-school programs. The Office of Safe and Healthy Students develops and disseminates materials about preventing domestic human trafficking, such as "Human Trafficking of Children in the United States: A Fact Sheet for Schools" and the Readiness and Emergency Management for Schools Web site. In addition, a guide for educators and administrators that will raise awareness, assist in identification, and support schools in developing intervention strategies and protocols is currently underway; the expected dissemination date is November 2013.

**Department of Homeland Security** (DHS): DHS consists of more than 20 component agencies and offices, including both law enforcement entities and the nation's immigration services. In 2010, DHS launched the Blue Campaign, a first-of-its-kind campaign to coordinate and enhance the Department's anti-human trafficking efforts. The Blue Campaign—which includes 17 DHS components, such as U.S. Immigration and Customs Enforcement, U.S. Citizenship and Immigration Services, U.S. Customs and

Border Protection, the U.S. Coast Guard, and the Federal Law Enforcement Training Center—harnesses and leverages the varied authorities and resources of the Department to deter human trafficking by increasing awareness, protecting victims, and contributing to a robust criminal justice response. As the largest investigative agency within DHS, U.S. Immigration and Customs Enforcement Homeland Security Investigations (HSI) conducts domestic and international investigations of human trafficking, child sex tourism, and forced child labor. Since the passage of the PROTECT Act of 2003, HSI has focused investigative resources on investigating U.S. citizens and lawful permanent residents that travel abroad to engage in illicit sexual activity with minors. Worldwide, HSI conducts law enforcement training and public awareness campaigns, such as Hidden in Plain Sight, as part of its outreach efforts. HSI also provides trafficking victims with short-term immigration relief, manages the HSI Victim Assistance Program, and operates a 24-hour hotline to report potential trafficking activity at 1-866-DHS-2-ICE. U.S. Citizenship and Immigration Services (USCIS) grants immigration relief to trafficking victims, while also conducting training for nongovernmental organizations and law enforcement. USCIS officers are trained to identify potential trafficking victims and to notify law enforcement personnel upon encountering such individuals. U.S. Customs and Border Protection (CBP) conducts public campaigns, such as No Te Engañes, to raise awareness among potential victims and vulnerable communities. CBP also screens unaccompanied alien children to identify human trafficking victims. The U.S. Coast Guard routinely conducts maritime operations independently and with other federal law enforcement agencies and international partners to combat illegal migration, including human trafficking. The Federal Law Enforcement Training Center provides human trafficking training to federal, state, local, campus, and tribal law enforcement officers throughout the United States. Additionally, human trafficking courses are delivered at several of the International Law Enforcement Academies including the academy in Gaborone, Botswana, which is managed by the Federal Law Enforcement Training Center. DHS is the chair of the Human Smuggling and Trafficking Center steering group in coordination with the Department of Justice and Department of State. The Center provides a mechanism to bring together federal agency representatives from the policy, law enforcement, intelligence, and diplomatic areas to work together on a full time basis to achieve increased effectiveness, and to convert intelligence into effective law enforcement and other action. For more information, please visit the DHS Blue Campaign webpage or the DHS Blue Campaign Facebook page.

**United States Agency for International Development** (USAID): USAID funds international programs that prevent trafficking, protect and assist victims, and support prosecutions through training for police and criminal justice personnel. USAID reinforces successful anti-trafficking initiatives by funding programs that support economic development, child protection, women's empowerment, good governance, education, health, and human rights. USAID supports individual country assessments of the scope and nature of trafficking and the efforts of government, civil society, and international organization to combat it.

**U.S. Equal Employment Opportunity Commission** (EEOC or Commission): The EEOC investigates, attempts to informally resolve, and litigates charges alleging discrimination on the basis of race, color, national origin, sex, religion, age, disability, and genetic information. In appropriate cases, therefore, the EEOC is able to secure civil remedies (e.g., monetary and equitable relief) for trafficking victims. In 2010, the EEOC participated for the first time in both the PITF and SPOG meetings as a full partner. On January 19, 2011, the Commission conducted a public meeting entitled on the Agency's Role in fighting human trafficking and forced labor (http://www.eeoc.gov/eeoc/meetings/1-19-11/transcript.cfm). The EEOC has committed to active participation in order to identify additional labor trafficking cases through its 53 offices nationwide.

# ANNEX C. THE HUMAN TRAFFICKING STORY IN NUMBERS

Global efforts to combat trafficking are hampered by lack of solid data. USAID and the USG as a whole, under the leadership of the White House, is investing in multiple efforts to address this challenge. This emphasis on empirical data is fully consistent with USAID Forward and the Agency's enhanced focus on M&E. However, various organizations track TIP data which may be useful to Missions. Some of these data, from the 2011-2012 timeframe, are listed below for reference.

- Number of Countries Around the World with Documented Cases of Trafficking in Persons:

  186[55]

- Estimated Number of Adults and Children in Forced Labor, Bonded Labor, and Forced Prostitution Around the World:

  20.9 million[56]

- Number of Victims World Wide Identified and Assisted in 2011:

  42,291[57]

- Number of Products or Services Produced by Child or Forced Labor:

  130 goods from 71 countries[58]

- The Dollars Earned Annually by Traffickers Buying and Selling People:

  $32,000,000,000[59]

- Amount Spent by USAID in 2011 to Combat TIP:

  $16,600,000[60]

- Percentage of Human Trafficking Cases in Which the Traffickers Were Known by the Victim:

  46%[61]

- The Estimated Percentage of Trafficking Victims who are Female:

  56%[62]

- Percentage of Sexual Exploitation Victims who are Women and Girls:

---

[55]DOS. 2012. *Trafficking in Persons Report.* Washington, D.C., 52.

[56]International Labour Organization (ILO). 2012. *"Global Estimate on Forced Labour Factsheet."* Geneva, Switzerland, June.

[57]DOS. 2012. *Trafficking in Persons Report.* Washington, D.C., 44.

[58]DOL. 2011. *List of Goods Produced by Child Labor or Forced Labor.* Washington, D.C. 27.

[59]ILO. 2009. *The Cost of Coercion* (Geneva, Switzerland).

[60]USAID. 2012. Counter Trafficking in Persons Policy. Washington, D.C., 4.

[61]International Organization for Migration (IOM). 1999. Counter-Trafficking Database, 78 Countries, 1999–2006.

[62]ILO. 2005. *A Global Alliance Against Forced Labor.* Geneva, Switzerland, 15.

98%[63]

- Number of Countries that have yet to Convict a Trafficker Under Laws in Compliance with the Palermo Protocol:

    62[64]

- Number of Successful Convictions for Labor Trafficking in 2011:

    278 out of 456 prosecutions[65]

---

[63]Ibid., 15.
[64]DOS. 2012. *Trafficking in Persons Report*, 30.
[65]Ibid., 44.

# ANNEX D. THE TRADE IN HUMANS—INFLUENCES OF SUPPLY AND DEMAND

Human trafficking is a commercial, for-profit activity that varies by country and region. A complex phenomenon, human trafficking is influenced by social, economic, cultural, and political factors. The economic concept of supply and demand is commonly used to describe the activity.

## Factors That Influence the Supply Side of Human Trafficking

Trafficking victims comprise the supply side of the equation. The supply of vulnerable individuals is influenced by economic, social, cultural, political, and environmental factors. Some of the risk factors that create vulnerability to human trafficking include the following:

- Poverty
- Corruption
- Weak rule of law
- Political oppression
- Lack of social and political opportunities
- Lack of human rights and/or discrimination based on caste, ethnicity, gender, religious affiliation, among other biases
- Lack of access to education and jobs
- Gender stratification
- Family disruptions (as seen in death resulting from armed conflict or HIV/AIDS, leaving children with no adult support)
- Family dysfunction (caused by drugs, alcohol, or violence) that leaves children outside of parental care and renders them particularly vulnerable
- Dislocation and/or danger caused by civil unrest, internal armed conflict, war, or militarism
- Economic disruptions to family finances caused by natural disasters (such a droughts or floods that cause a rural family to be without food stocks or income) or environmental degradation
- Domestic violence (driving women and children to run away and live in the streets)
- Institutional factors (such as the failure of the State to register the children of the poor—in such cases, the State cannot keep track of the children's welfare)
- Presence of traffickers, recruiters, loan sharks, and other predatory individuals within a community

Vulnerability can change over time, often as a result of the confluence of factors listed above.

Poverty alone does not necessarily create vulnerability to trafficking, but when combined with other factors (such as civil unrest), these can lead to higher risk for being trafficked. This phenomenon is referred to as "poverty-plus," where a plus factor (such as the illness of a parent) can serve as a trigger and increase vulnerability of the poor.

Women and girls can be especially vulnerable, due to social, economic and political inequities, including unequal access to education and employment opportunities. There is also a strong indication that traffickers and exploitative employers tend to recruit victims from regions with large-scale emigration. Due to this increased level of vulnerability, awareness campaigns and other anti-trafficking policies should be targeted to areas where migration flows are high.

Seasonal workers, widows, informal sector laborers, refugees and internally displaced persons—many of whom are dislocated en masse by conflict or natural disasters—are particularly vulnerable to exploitation and abuse through forced labor and trafficking. Traffickers target refugee and Internally Displaced Person (IDP) camps in order to exploit vulnerabilities of individuals who have lost their homes or who have been separated from their families and support systems. Unaccompanied minors and child-led households are some of the most vulnerable populations, but traffickers look for any individual lacking protective environments. Camps have also been sites of exploitation by aid workers and security forces who have demanded sex, money, and services in return for assistance.

## Factors That Influence the Demand Side of Human Trafficking

Defining demand is highly complex. The United Nations organizes the demand for labor or sex trafficking into three categories:

- Employer demand: employers; owners; managers; or subcontractors;

- Consumer demand: clients (in the sex industry); corporate buyers (in manufacturing); household members (in domestic work); and

- Third party enabling: recruiters; agents; transporters; and others who participate knowingly in the movement of persons for the purpose of exploitation.[66]

In the case of labor trafficking, consumers often provide the demand, and thus the profit incentive, to the traffickers. Consumers can include companies that subcontract certain types of services, end-consumers who buy cheap goods produced by trafficking victims, or individuals who use the services of trafficking victims. By changing our purchasing choices and asking questions about how our products were made, consumers can reduce these types of demand and help stem human trafficking. In an effort to increase public awareness of trafficking, DOS provided funding to develop an Internet tool called the Slavery Footprint (www.slaveryfootprint.org) through which individual consumers can find out if they are purchasing goods or services through organizations that use forced labor.

Demand for sex trafficking is generated by consumers who purchase sex acts, as well as traffickers, brothel owners, and corrupt officials who derive profit from the sale of sex. Secondary profiteers include businesses that provide support services to the sex industry, including hotels, restaurants, and transport. Although there is debate in the academic and civil society community about this trend, some studies have also linked trafficking to large sporting events.[67] The high number of attendees can increase demand, with

---

[66]UNODC Toolkit to Combat Trafficking in Persons 9.12, http://www.unodc.org/documents/human-trafficking/Toolkit-files/08-58296_tool_9-12.pdf; And ILO. 2006. *Demand Side of Human Trafficking in Asia: Empirical Findings.* Bangkok, Thailand.
http://www.ilo.org/public/english/region/asro/bangkok/library/download/pub06-01.pdf.

[67]Melissa Beale. 2011. "The Infamous Link Between Sex Trafficking, Sex Tourism, and Sporting Events—What Lies Ahead for Brazil." Washington, D.C.: Council on Hemispheric Affairs. http://www.coha.org/the-infamous-link-between-sex-trafficking-sex-tourism-and-sporting-events-%E2%80%93-what-lies-ahead-for-brazil/, 2011. And Julie Ham. 2011. *What's the Cost of a Rumor: A Guide to Sorting Out the Myths and the Facts About Sporting Events and Trafficking.* Bangkok, Thailand: Global Alliance Against Traffic in Women. And http://www.gaatw.org/publications/WhatstheCostofaRumour.11.15.2011.pdf. And Carl Bialik. 2010. "The Illusive

---

COUNTER-TRAFFICKING IN PERSONS FIELD GUIDE

traffickers luring victims to the site with promises of legitimate work around the games or by using special tourist visas to disguise them as spectators.

In conflict and post-conflict areas, displaced and endangered people make desperate decisions, including relying on smugglers (who may turn out to be traffickers) in an attempt to get out of harm's way. In recent years, there have been examples of women fleeing the conflict in Kosovo, of children exploited in the refugee camps in East and West Timor, and increasingly, of Colombians victimized in the trafficking "market." A number of reports have documented increases in sex trafficking in and around military installations and in places with a substantial UN peacekeeper presence.[68] To address that phenomenon and the links to the contractor community that have been documented, USAID established an internal "C–TIP Contractor Compliance Working Group" that produced the Standard Operating Procedure on Contractor Compliance.[69]

As part of USAID's implementation of the 2011 United States National Action Plan on Women, Peace, and Security, USAID will increase its efforts to combat trafficking in a few specific conflict and crisis-affected countries. The criteria for selecting these countries, both through the National Action Plan and the C–TIP Policy, include but are not limited to: significant U.S. government investment; multiyear international deployments with a significant number (such as over 10,000) of personnel deployed; and opportunities to build partnerships with other donors or stakeholders. In addition to new Agency-wide training on ethical standards related to the C–TIP Code of Conduct, USAID will provide training and technical assistance to personnel in selected Missions to design, implement, monitor, and evaluate effective C–TIP interventions in conflict-affected areas. USAID, led by the C–TIP Champions and the Resident Legal Advisors assigned to Missions in conflict and crisis-affected areas will educate civilian contractors and aid workers on the prevention of TIP in crisis and conflict-affected environments.

## Additional Factors That Contribute to Human Trafficking

Several additional factors contribute to human trafficking, including the following:

- Growing restrictions on legal immigration: In the face of increasing restrictions on legal immigration to destination countries, many migrants willfully ignore the associated risks of human trafficking and resort to alien smugglers for assistance.

- Treating human trafficking victims as criminals: Many victims are reluctant to cooperate with law enforcement to prosecute offenders because of the practice of treating victims as criminals and the fear of retribution due to insufficient witness protection programs. Legal and administrative penalties imposed on TIP victims as a direct result of their enslavement further violate their rights and obstruct efforts to identify and prosecute traffickers.

- Lack of political will: Insufficient commitment to enforce existing legislation or mandates derails C–TIP efforts in many locations. Notwithstanding the number of countries that have ratified the

Link Between Sex Trafficking and Sporting Events." *Wall Street Journal*, June 18. *And* Jana Hennig. 2006. *Trafficking in Human Beings and the 2006 World Cup in Germany.* Geneva, Switzerland: IOM. http://www.iom.ch/jahia/webdav/shared/shared/mainsite/projects/documents/World_Cup_2006_CT_Draft_Report.pdf.

[68]Michael J. Jordan. 2004. "Sex Charges Haunt UN Forces: In Places Like Congo and Kosovo Peacekeepers Have Been Accused of Abusing the People They're Protecting." *Christian Science Monitor* .http://www.csmonitor.com/2004/1126/p06s02-wogi.html, November 26. And Emily Wax. 2005. "Congo's Desperate One-Dollar UN Girls." *Washington Post.*,http://www.washingtonpost.com/wp-dyn/articles/A52333-2005Mar20.html, March 25.

[69]Standard Operating Procedure available at http://transition.usaid.gov/policy/C-TIP_SOP.pdf.

major conventions and adopted C–TIP legislation, enforcement and ensuring accountability remain uneven compared with the scope of the problem. Governments may deny or ignore the problem and withhold assistance to TIP victims required under the Palermo Protocol.

- Corruption: Government officials, police, border guards, and labor inspectors often accept bribes and collude with offenders in the selling of fake documentation. In some cases, current or former military or police personnel operate brothels or sites of prostitution. Some are also customers who warn brothel owners in advance of a raid or enforcement action. Moreover, some convicted traffickers are able to avoid serving prison sentences by paying bribes to officials.

- Weak law enforcement: Efforts to combat human trafficking are often hindered by inadequate law enforcement capacity. Many countries do not have comprehensive C–TIP legislation, as required under the Palermo Protocol. Human trafficking penalties are often weak, especially compared with penalties for other criminal activities such as drug and arms trafficking.

- Globalization and increased sophistication of international organized crime: International criminals have exploited the ease with which goods, money, and people now flow across international borders. The globalization of the world's economy has increased human migration, both legal and illegal.

- Social custom of entrusting children to the care of more affluent friends or relatives: In some countries, parents entrust their children to the care of affluent friends or family members in the hope that their children will receive an education and/or improve their chances in life. These children can end up in situations of domestic servitude and are vulnerable to physical and sexual abuse. In some cases, parents sell their children for financial remuneration.

- Social devaluation of women and girls and other form of prejudice: Vulnerability of women and girls can be increased due to their low social and political standing and a related lack of economic, social, educational, and political opportunities. Some females are placed at increased risk due to the practice of forced marriage. In addition, prejudice based on race and other factors can contribute to the exploitation of migrant workers and other vulnerable individuals and groups.

- Poor governance: Forced labor situations can arise as a result of a series of labor market failures and a weak State capacity to effectively regulate labor markets and migration flows. In particular, the failure of the government to adequately regulate the labor recruitment industry has led to gross abuses that contribute to the trafficking of workers. Exorbitant or illegal recruitment fees, recruitment expenses illegally shifted to workers, and other unscrupulous recruitment practices can result in workers' involuntary servitude.

Effective interventions call for governments not only to punish forced labor as a penal offense but also to step in and effectively regulate the economy thereby creating more options for decent work in the formal economy. Regarding the many vulnerable workers in the informal economy and "invisible" places of employment (i.e., sweatshops and brothels), effective strategies to combat TIP involve working jointly with community-based organizations, trade unions, labor inspectors, and law enforcement.

## How Readily Are Trafficking Victims Identified? What Happens to Those Victims Who Fall Through the Cracks?

Most trafficked persons go unidentified and are vulnerable to further victimization, as they may be punished by law enforcement officials for acts committed as a direct result of their having been trafficked. After they leave a trafficking situation, many remain in the informal sector as undocumented, unregistered individuals. Unable to access protection and assistance services, or contribute to the investigation and prosecution of traffickers, trafficked persons remain vulnerable to repeated exploitation and re-trafficking.

Often male victims of trafficking—both adult men and boys—get overlooked due to common misconceptions that human trafficking only affects women and girls.

# ANNEX E. THE TRADE IN HUMANS — THE ACTORS INVOLVED

Human traffickers recruit, transport, harbor, or receive persons through the use of force, coercion, abduction, fraud, deception or other means for the purpose of exploitation. A range of actors—including recruiters, intermediaries, document providers, transporters, corrupt officials, service providers, and employers of trafficked persons—support the act of human trafficking. An individual may take part in one or multiple parts of the TIP process. Traffickers include organized crime networks or individuals who are part of the community of the trafficked person, such as neighbors or family members, acting alone or in collaboration with one or two accomplices.

## Organized Criminal Groups

Organized criminal groups, characterized by defined hierarchical structures, continue their involvement in the buying and selling of humans. Typically the boss (an individual, family, or tight-knit group) operates in a way that insulates him or her from lower tier operators. A document forger, for instance, may not know who is at the top and will thus not be in a position to share this information if arrested.

Another dominant model is the network model in which organized criminal groups work together in a decentralized way, with each group controlling a specific, specialized area. These specialists may collaborate regularly or on an ad hoc basis. Moreover, specialists may support several different criminal networks. Maximization of profit is the overall goal, and transactions resemble those in other business models. Networks may cooperate with one another if cooperation is financially beneficial to all.

## Individual or Small-Scale Trafficking Operations

Human trafficking can also involve informal participants or individuals who perform a single service, such as recruitment. These individuals may include friends or family members of the trafficked person. A boyfriend may force his partner into a situation of commercial sexual exploitation. An aunt may make money by selling her niece or nephew to traffickers. A friend of the family may deceive an individual into following a false promise of work or education. These individuals may work regularly or on an *ad hoc* basis.

## Evolving Role of Technology

Evidence indicates that traffickers are increasingly using technology, such as online classified ads, social networking fora, and SMS texting, to lure, recruit and manipulate victims. Brothel-based operations are becoming more mobile, making victim identification even more difficult than before. The potential for the spread of trafficking activity through technology is vast but so are the solutions for C–TIP. Millions of individuals use social networking sites and, as of 2010, there are more than 2 billion Internet users worldwide. Youth are among the most vulnerable to trafficking and the most likely to use the Internet and mobile phones. For more information on the link between TIP and technology, please refer to the Additional Resources Annex.

# ANNEX F. MONITORING AND EVALUATION CONSIDERATIONS FOR C–TIP INTEGRATION

As a cross-cutting issue, dedicated C–TIP projects can combine programming elements from each of the functional sectors, as demonstrated in the Results Framework. Programming to prevent TIP, for example, could involve legislative reform, anti-corruption, civil society engagement, agricultural programming, economic growth or education elements depending upon the country context. Likewise, the Protection Objective could engage medical caregivers, law enforcement and justice sector actors, as well as policymakers.

Although the majority of USAID C–TIP programs to date have been stand-alone programs, the 2012 C–TIP Policy prioritizes an integrated approach in order to maximize USAID's programmatic reach. Project designs for economic growth programs in some countries should address the likelihood of forced or child labor in sectors such as manufacturing and agricultural where the incidence rate is most prevalent. Health programs may incorporate the unique medical and psychological needs of VoTs as a discrete target beneficiary. Similarly, in countries where sex trafficking is prevalent, HIV/AIDS programming should consider ways to reach these VoTs. The chart below lists various examples of how C–TIP elements could be integrated into diverse programs.

## FEED THE FUTURE

| OJECT PURPOSE | POTENTIAL C–TIP ACTIVITY | PERFORMANCE INDICATORS |
|---|---|---|
| Promote agricultural production | Prevent child trafficking in agriculture | % of farm laborers are children is lowered |
| | | Laws regulating use of child labor in conformity with international standards |
| | | % of target group (rural children ) who stay enrolled in school |
| Incorporate international human rights standards into domestic agricultural policy. | Work with government and civil society to assess impact of agricultural policy on immigration dynamics | # of policies that mitigate negative effects on migrant/undocumented workers or other vulnerable populations |

## ECONOMIC GROWTH/PRIVATE ENTERPRISE

| PROJECT PURPOSE | POTENTIAL C–TIP ACTIVITY | PERFORMANCE INDICATORS |
|---|---|---|
| Promote economic growth/SMEs. | Increase social and economic opportunities for vulnerable persons in source communities | % of targeted vulnerable persons employed, enrolled, or participating in micro-credit schemes |
| | | # of businesses participating in employment programs for vulnerable groups |
| | Support adoption of economic policy that fairly regulates labor immigration. | # of policies that mitigate negative effects on vulnerable populations |
| Increase capacity of labor unions, labor inspectors, and government officials to develop and implement protective labor regulations | Train labor inspectors, union leaders and government officials on TIP issues and how to identify TIP | # of labor inspectors, union leaders and government officials trained and knowledgeable on trafficking issues |
| | | % of VoTs identified by labor inspectors, labor unions, and government officials that receive direct assistance |
| | Build capacity of unions to provide safety net for most vulnerable | # of unions providing outreach/services to those most vulnerable to TIP |
| | Work with government to develop and implement regulations for safe labor migration | # of recruitment agencies in compliance with C–TIP regulations |

## EDUCATION

| PROJECT PURPOSE | POTENTIAL C–TIP ACTIVITY | PERFORMANCE INDICATORS |
|---|---|---|
| Promote higher graduation rates in primary education | Institutionalize C–TIP curriculum in primary school education | True/Yes |
| | Train teachers on TIP and their role in preventing it | # of teachers trained |
| | | % of vulnerable persons graduate |
| Promote vocational training | Provide vocational training and placement opportunities for vulnerable groups, including VoTs | % of vulnerable persons to get jobs |

## GLOBAL HEALTH

| OJECT PURPOSE | POTENTIAL C–TIP ACTIVITY | PERFORMANCE INDICATORS |
|---|---|---|
| Improve quality and accessibility of medical treatment and care | Train healthcare providers and substance abuse counselors on TIP, including symptoms of VoTs and special care needs | % of healthcare providers who have received specialized training |
| | | Level of satisfaction of VoTs who received medical assistance |
| Mainstream rights-based approach to medical services | Capacity building at national and local levels to mainstream C–TIP prevention and protection activities | # C–TIP policies adopted |

## MEDIA

| PROJECT PURPOSE | POTENTIAL C–TIP ACTIVITY | PERFORMANCE INDICATORS |
|---|---|---|
| Enhance capacity of media to report accurately and professionally | Train journalists on TIP | # journalists trained |
| | | # of accurate and discrete instances of media coverage on TIP issues |
| Promote use of social media to promote social policy | Build awareness campaigns on C–TIP around large events such as a sporting event, concert, etc. | # C–TIP campaigns using social media |

## CONFLICT/CRISIS/DISASTER ZONES

| PROJECT PURPOSE | POTENTIAL C–TIP ACTIVITY | PERFORMANCE INDICATORS |
|---|---|---|
| Provide appropriate and comprehensive direct assistance to conflict victims | Establish SOPs/Guidelines for identification and sheltering of VoTs | True/Yes |
| | | # of VoTs identified using SOPs/guidelines and referred for services |
| | | # of VoTs removed from detention facilities |
| | | % of re/integrated VoTs employed, re/inserted in education system, etc. |
| Promote protection of human rights | C–TIP training for human rights defenders | # trained |
| | Public information campaigns to raise awareness of TIP in conflict zones | % increase in # of citizens who are aware of TIP issues |
| Promote protection/resiliency of vulnerable populations | Work with governments and civil society to ensure consideration of C–TIP implications in disaster risk reduction and humanitarian assistance policies | # of C–TIP policies that address most vulnerable populations |

## GLOBAL CLIMATE CHANGE (GCC)

| PROJECT PURPOSE | POTENTIAL C–TIP ACTIVITY | PERFORMANCE INDICATORS |
|---|---|---|
| Promote protection of those displaced or made vulnerable by GCC | C-TIP awareness for communities whose livelihoods have been negatively affected by GCC | # of awareness campaigns |
| | Work with local research institution to collect data on demographics of affected populations | # of studies that identify GCC-related migration/TIP dynamics |

## CIVIL SOCIETY

| PROJECT PURPOSE | POTENTIAL C–TIP ACTIVITY | PERFORMANCE INDICATORS |
|---|---|---|
| Empower local civil society organizations to promote social policy | Provide technical and organizational capacity building support to C–TIP NGOs | # of NGOs effectively advocating for TIP prevention and protection |

# ANNEX G. ILLUSTRATIVE RESULTS FRAMEWORK—THE 4PS PARADIGM

## Prevention

**DEVELOPMENT OBJECTIVE 1:** Comprehensive measures to prevent all forms of TIP are established and institutionalized

| RECRUITING AND LABOR PRACTICES | VULNERABLE INDIVIDUALS AND GROUPS | ANTI-CORRUPTION | DEMAND REDUCTION |
|---|---|---|---|
| IR 1.1: Appropriate controls over labor recruitment and working conditions adopted and implemented | IR 1.2: Decreased engagement in high risk behaviors and expanded economic and educational opportunities as alternatives to TIP | IR 1.3: Corrupt practices that facilitate trafficking reduced | IR 1.4: Demand for goods or services produced or provided by trafficked persons reduced |
| 1.1.1: Licensing and regulatory controls over recruitment/ sponsoring agencies (or individual recruiting agents) developed (or strengthened) and enforced | 1.2.1: Potential victims and their families, educators and community leaders informed of the risks and perils of trafficking and instruction provided on how to decrease that risk | 1.3.1: Capacity of governmental agencies to expose, investigate, and prosecute instances of corruption facilitating TIP increased | 1.4.1: Public informed of the incidence of TIP in production of certain goods or services |
| 1.1.2: Minimum labor standards enforced | 1.2.2: Expanded economic and educational opportunities for vulnerable populations, as alternatives to TIP created | 1.3.2: Transparency of governmental practices related to TIP increased by civil society activism and open government initiatives | 1.4.2: Commercial sex users informed of the correlation between commercial sex and trafficking |

| RECRUITING AND LABOR PRACTICES | VULNERABLE INDIVIDUALS AND GROUPS | ANTI-CORRUPTION | DEMAND REDUCTION |
|---|---|---|---|
| 1.1.3: Official or voluntary monitoring networks ensure compliance with licensing and labor standards | | | 1.4.3: Employers in industries known to utilize forced and child labor proactively oppose all forms of TIP |
| 1.1.4: The establishment (or strengthening) of incentives that encourage employers to keep their employees—and encourage employees to remain—in the formal labor sector supported | | | |

## Protection

**DEVELOPMENT OBJECTIVE 2:** Victim-centered services to provide protection and assistance to trafficked persons and to meet special needs of child victims of trafficking are established and sustainable

| VICTIM SERVICES | REPATRIATION and REINTEGRATION | SPECIAL NEEDS OF CHILD VICTIMS OF TRAFFICKING | LAW ENFORCEMENT/POLICE INTERACTION |
|---|---|---|---|
| IR 2.1: System of specialized comprehensive and non-discriminatory services for VoTs established and maintained | IR 2.2: Voluntary repatriation and reintegration processes available to victims of trafficking in line with international standards | IR 2.3: The special needs of child victims of trafficking included in a comprehensive victim assistance framework | IR 2.4: Law enforcement entities enhance protection of trafficked persons |
| 2.1.1: Systematic procedures guide first responders in the process of victim identification | 2.2.1: Rights-based procedures in destination countries ensure VoTs not deported inappropriately or punished for crimes associated with being trafficked, such as prostitution or illegal migration and have legal alternatives to removal to countries where they may face retribution or hardship | 2.3.1: Laws and procedures to identify child victims of forced labor and trafficking strengthened | 2.4.1: Law enforcement entities and local communities facilitate victim identification and protection |

| 2.1.2: Basic services for survivors of trafficking available, including counseling, shelter, security, food, legal services and where appropriate, vocational or job training | 2.2.2: Countries of origin and destination mutually employ practices for safe and voluntary repatriation and reintegration of trafficked persons | 2.3.2: Facilities and services to effectively address the special needs of child victims of trafficking established and/or enhanced | 2.4.2: Capacity of law enforcement to assist trafficked persons in accessing social services increased |
|---|---|---|---|
| 2.1.3: Access to justice for survivors of trafficking increased | 2.2.3: Systematic reintegration procedures in countries of origin protect trafficked persons against exploitation and re-trafficking | 2.3.3: Legal needs of child VoTs during trials against traffickers adequately met | |
| | 2.2.4: Social/cultural stigma associated with VoTs mitigated | | |

## Prosecution

### DEVELOPMENT OBJECTIVE 3: Prosecution of those willfully engaged in TIP strengthened, resulting in increased convictions and sentencing[70]

| JUSTICE SYSTEM | SUPPORT AND WITNESS PROTECTION PROGRAMS |
|---|---|
| IR 3.1: Justice systems capable of effectively, fairly, and efficiently handling TIP cases | IR 3.2: Safety and protection of trafficked persons institutionalized throughout legal proceedings |
| 3.1.1: Administrative procedures promote processing of TIP cases | 3.2.1: Victim rights protected in the course of legal proceedings |
| 3.1.2: Law enforcement's capacity to investigate TIP cases and support prosecution of traffickers increased | 3.2.2: Victims provided for and protected after trial as feasible |

[70]While prosecution programs are critical to effectively combating TIP, in line with USAID's C–TIP Policy, the Agency will leverage its comparative advantage by focusing on investments on protection, prevention, and partnership. The U.S. Departments of State and Justice continue to invest in prosecution programs—where their experience and expertise lies.

# Partnerships

**DEVELOPMENT OBJECTIVE 4: A global movement dedicated to the eradication of all forms of TIP collectively and productively supported by governments, civil society, and private sector**

| NATIONAL COORDINATION | DATA COLLECTION | INTERNATIONAL COOPERATION | PUBLIC-PRIVATE PARTNERSHIPS and INTRAGOVERNMENTAL PARTNERSHIPS |
|---|---|---|---|
| IR 4.1: NRM and/or NAP coherently coordinate C–TIP activities effectively | IR 4.2: Reliable data on TIP activity effectively collected and shared among interested governmental and non-governmental parties | IR 4.3: Legal and voluntary mechanisms supporting international, intergovernmental and regional collaboration and partnerships to effectively combat cross-border trafficking adopted (or strengthened) and utilized | IR 4.4: Establishment of partnerships between both public and private entities/donors and within the U.S. government |
| 4.1.1: A comprehensive NRM and/or NAP delineates referral strategies or establishes actions to provide support and protection services for trafficked persons developed or strengthened | 4.2.1 : Capacity to measure incidence of TIP developed or strengthened | 4.3.1: Relevant international instruments ratified | 4.4.1: Private companies establish PPPs and CSR programs to combat TIP |
| 4.1.2: A coordinating mechanism effectively reviews performance of NRM or oversees implementation of the NAP | 4.2.2: Integrity and utility of TIP data increased | 4.3.2: Increased government capacity to implement international instruments | 4.4.2:USG collaboration strengthened internally to combat TIP |
| 4.1.3: The NRM and/or NAP effectively implemented | 4.2.3: Formal mechanism established (or strengthened) to share TIP data or information with relevant entities within and across national borders | 4.3.3: Cross-border and regional networks facilitate widespread awareness raising, identification, care, repatriation and reintegration of victims, cross-border investigations, and services | |

# Prevention

## Development Objective 1: Comprehensive measures to prevent all forms of TIP are established and institutionalized

In the field of counter-trafficking, prevention activities have primarily taken the form of public education and awareness campaigns directed at populations vulnerable to trafficking as well as first responders, such as social workers and police. Too often, these campaigns have been designed absent quality survey data and with no measurement of impact. Prevention strategies will improve when informed by reliable, replicable data.

While public education and awareness programs are critical to combating trafficking, they are not the only prevention strategies. Prevention efforts can also include programs to increase the capacity of vulnerable populations and first responders to take proactive steps to prevent trafficking and projects to address the root causes of trafficking, such as the absence of educational or employment opportunities or the presence of gender and ethnic discrimination. Leveraging awareness programs by integrating tools through which individuals can take steps against trafficking, for example, is a more robust prevention approach. An awareness campaign that also provides guidance to communities on how to form neighborhood counter-trafficking vigilance committees to report and investigate suspected cases is one example. An economic growth program that provides vocational and livelihoods training to potential trafficking victims to reduce their vulnerability is another example. These prevention strategies embrace a multi-layered "pro-poor" integrated approach to create an environment where trafficking is challenged. Such an approach reflects increased understanding of trafficking in both the formal and informal labor markets and the need for transparency and monitoring in corporate supply chains to prevent corruption. [71] The IRs under this objective work together to prevent TIP by regulating and monitoring formal market sectors, strengthening vulnerable populations, curbing public corruption in TIP, and reducing the demand for commercial sex and cheap labor.

### Recruiting and Labor Practices

### IR 1.1: Appropriate controls over labor recruitment and working conditions adopted and implemented

*Issue:* Traffickers can lure victims into forced labor situations within a particular country or can recruit them from abroad. Typically victims are lured through promises of legitimate work, often presenting the appearance of a credible employment agency or a trusted friend. Fraudulent contracts, passports, and visa documentation can buttress the appearance of legitimacy. Similarly, fraudulent documentation creates the impression of a legitimate labor force, sometimes fooling even the businesses employing the trafficked labor. In addition, high and illegal recruitment fees are exploitive recruitment practices that can lead to situations of debt bondage. Victims themselves are prevented from reporting their conditions through physical restraint, threats of repercussion, or lack of knowledge. Language barriers may also pose challenges to reporting.

Labor standards in small enterprises and the informal labor sector can be especially difficult to enforce. Workers in the informal sector, such as individuals recruited as domestic servants in households or as laborers on fishing boats or small farms, are particularly vulnerable to trafficking.

*Possible Performance Indicators at the IR level:*

---

[71] For a discussion of pro-poor growth and addressing vulnerability, see Organisation for Economic Cooperation and Development. 2009. *Promoting Pro-Poor Growth Social Protection.* http://www.oecd.org/dataoecd/63/10/43514563.pdf..

---

- Percent of targeted improvements to labor recruitment regulation implemented
- Percent of targeted improvements to procedures for labor inspections implemented
- Number of labor inspections conducted in targeted industries with suspected high levels of trafficking

**Illustrative Activities:**

*1.1.1: Develop (or strengthen) and enforce rigorous licensing and regulatory controls over recruitment and sponsoring agencies or individual agents through:*

- Licensing of business entities seeking to engage in hiring (either as recruiting or sponsoring agencies) to include background checks of principals and verification of business financing and contact information.[72] Individual recruiters should be targeted in addition to companies and/or agencies. A significant part of exploitive recruitment practices involves individual, unlicensed recruiters who make fraudulent offers and charge illegal fees to villagers or other vulnerable segments of the population.

- Stringent regulation of business practices which includes requirements to prominently display a valid business license and provide prospective workers with trafficking warnings and instructions on how to report to law enforcement. Other regulations should require making contracts available in the prospective worker's native language; informing workers of the process for reporting sexual or physical abuse; maintaining placement files with a copy of the worker's passport, visa, and contracts for each recruited individual; advising prospective workers of their right to consult an attorney or other advisor prior to signing contracts; providing contact information for the entity with whom the employment relationship is envisioned; and providing a statement of worker rights and labor standards.

*Possible Activity Indicators:*

- Licensing requirements updated to include background checks, financing and contact verification (Y/N)
- Number of labor/employment agencies licensed under updated criteria
- Percent of labor/employment agencies displaying business licenses and trafficking warnings
- Percent of labor/employment agencies complying with newly implemented best practice regulations such as contracts in native language and advising prospective workers of their rights

*1.1.2: Develop (or strengthen) and enforce international labor standards by:*

- Ensuring that national laws and regulations are consistent with international norms and the country's own labor laws (assuming that existing labor laws are well developed), setting clear limitations on the number of hours, establishing wage rates, requiring safe working conditions free from the use of child and forced labor, and prohibiting employers or recruiters from withholding workers' passports.

---

[72]"Sponsoring agencies" are typically logistical facilitators in destination countries, arranging for travel documentation, transit, housing, and employment placement for trafficked workers. Trafficking schemes often involve the recruiter, the sponsoring agency, and the employer, although in some instances the employer simply contracts with the sponsoring agency for temporary laborers at market value and is unaware of the exploitative relationship.

- Requiring businesses to register employment of foreign nationals. Follow-up inspections should include spot verification of the authenticity of the worker's travel documentation and employment permit. Confidential interviews with random workers should confirm that conditions of employment comply with minimum labor standards.

- Prohibiting employers from obtaining, and holding for any period, the travel documents of their foreign national employees. Such documentation includes passports, visas, and other documents permitting the employees to travel and remain in the host country.

- Utilizing formal monitoring mechanisms of licensed entities, including verifying the legitimacy of positions filled and confirming authenticity of documentation in placement files.

- Training labor inspectors to identify cases of TIP during the course of regular workplace inspections.

- Criminalizing the exchange of a child's labor in payment of a debt.

- Prohibiting the exchange of an individual's labor in payment of a debt in the absence of a contract specifying a reasonable, pre-determined date when the debt will be paid off by the labor and the laborer may exit the agreement.

- Partnering with government and civil society to ensure that laws and regulations pertaining to establishing and registering businesses, obtaining permits and certifications, etc. are consistent with international norms and are enforced. This may be done through collaborations with host government law enforcement mechanisms.

*Possible Activity Indicators:*

➢ Number of labor inspectors trained to identify trafficking cases[73]
➢ Policies and procedures for labor inspections developed through a participatory process (with police and labor inspectorate) that forms the foundation for inspection techniques training
➢ Number of trainers trained to deliver new curricula
➢ Percent of labor inspectors trained on improved inspection techniques who pass follow-up test one year after training
➢ Number of follow-up confidential interviews conducted by labor inspectors with random workers

*1.1.3: Develop (or strengthen) either official or voluntary monitoring networks (depending on the country context) ensuring compliance with labor standards licensing through:*

- Self-regulation and codes of conduct by employment agencies and businesses, especially in low-wage or manual labor industries known to utilize trafficked labor (i.e. mining, hospitality, entertainment, construction, domestic work, manufacturing, agriculture).

- Civil society and media monitoring of employment and sponsoring agencies and companies, as well as individual recruiters. While monitoring of private enterprise has limitations, the existence and authenticity of public documents, including licensing of employment agencies and issuance of work permits is possible where reasonable access-to-information laws exist. NGOs and journalists can also verify employment conditions by interviewing willing workers.

- Strengthened unions and worker organizations that safeguard members and reach out to non-unionized workplaces and publicize rights. This includes the implementation of workplace

---

[73]For USAID personnel in the field, this indicator could count toward the (DOS/USAID) F (budget) indicators: Number of people in host country trained on TIP-related issues.

mechanisms that allow workers to report on individuals who are vulnerable to exploitation, feeding such information into reporting processes in a NAP.

*Possible Activity Indicators:*

➤ Number of companies participating in self-regulation
➤ Number of companies adopting codes of conduct addressing TIP
➤ Number of trafficking-related violations identified by civil society and/or media and/or unions

*1.1.4: Support the establishment (or strengthening) of incentives that encourage employers to keep their employees—and encourage employees to remain—in the formal labor sector with:*

- Preferred tax treatment rewarding companies that create/provide legitimate jobs in the formal sector.

- Streamlined business regulation processes that enable employers to easily register.

- Labor laws that significantly restrict informal employment. Employees in the informal labor market are generally at greater risk of being trafficked or exploited.[74]

*Possible Activity Indicators:*

➤ Number of incentives established or strengthened that encourage workers to reside in the formal sector (quality of incentives should be assessed)
➤ Increase in formal employment for which those vulnerable to trafficking have relevant skills

*Measurement Approach:* At the IR level, measurement of whether controls over labor recruitment and employment of foreign nationals have been adopted and implemented is relatively straightforward. Adoption and implementation of those controls targeted by the intervention can be measured directly.

One challenge with measuring progress in the area of enforcement of minimum labor standards is the difficulty of interpreting data on changes in the number of trafficking cases identified by labor inspectors. Better-trained inspectors would be expected to identify more trafficking cases, at least initially. However, as the deterrent effect of improved inspections takes hold, and other anti-trafficking measures begin to have impact, the number of trafficking cases that will be identified may drop. (This may be in some cases because traffickers move their operations elsewhere as a result of increased labor inspections.) Thus, while it is important to track the total number of trafficking cases identified by inspectors, it is best to use the data as a contextual indicator rather than an actual performance indicator.

*Sustainability:* Codifying minimum labor standards and incorporating C–TIP measures into business regulation, creates an excellent framework that can guide other interventions indefinitely. Moreover, businesses are increasingly motivated to combat TIP through Corporate Social Responsibility (CSR) initiatives and codes of conduct. Ethical and legitimate companies compete with traffickers who promise outlandish salaries. Similarly, companies complying with international labor standards are disadvantaged by competitors who use slave labor to keep production costs low. As businesses and labor unions are increasingly engaged in monitoring workplaces and supply chains against TIP, these efforts will work to enhance the traditional public regulation of workplaces and compliance with national labor laws.

---

[74]Note that while this is generally a good practice, it is important to be sensitive to the fact that some informal sector workers, such as women who, for a variety of reasons, wish to conceal from their husbands that they are working, may not want their jobs to be formalized.

*Special Considerations:* Legislation prohibiting labor trafficking is less widespread than that addressing sex trafficking. Accordingly, interventions may need to be premised on the development (or strengthening) of a labor code that incorporates international labor standards and C–TIP regulation. Enforcement of labor standards will be complicated by the substantial informal sectors that characterize many of the economies in countries of origin and, to a lesser extent, destination countries. Similarly, cultural practices and economic necessities that engage children in family farms and businesses would likely be excluded from labor standards, creating opportunities to conceal trafficking schemes with a guise of familial labor. Where workers' rights and licensing requirements exist, or are developed, they should be incorporated into civic education materials informing vulnerable populations of their rights and providing them with a means of identifying fraudulent recruiters.

## Vulnerable Individuals and Groups

### IR 1.2: Decreased engagement in high risk behaviors and expanded economic and educational opportunities as alternatives to TIP

*Issue:* Lack of economic alternatives makes people vulnerable to all forms of trafficking. Internal trafficking often targets vulnerable children and youth for exploitation largely within the informal sector. Some victims are duped by promises of legitimate employment opportunities, while others agree to what they know will be onerous working conditions, believing that they will be able to earn money and return home at will. Family and community members are frequently involved in the recruitment process, often unaware of the true nature of the situation but sometimes complicit with the traffickers. Moreover, traffickers capitalize on situations that make it difficult to account for people, including internal displacement following conflict and natural disasters, and they target undocumented populations such as Roma, runaways, and orphans.

*Possible Performance Indicators at the IR level include*

➤ Percentage increase in household incomes among vulnerable households

➤ Percentage increase in enrollment rates in educational institutions among vulnerable populations

**Illustrative Activities**

*1.2.1: Inform potential victims and their families, educators and community leaders of the risks and perils of trafficking and instruction as to how to decrease that risk with:*

- Public information and/or social marketing campaigns drawing on public opinion survey data that inform potential victims and their families, educators and community leaders of the risks and perils of trafficking. Depending of the cultural context, consider various forms of conveying C–TIP information such as street theater, art displays, fairs or other events that draw large crowds.

- Trafficking prevention programs at orphanages, schools, sport clubs and community centers in areas particularly targeted by traffickers. Training can include local TIP patterns, trends, and recruitment strategies (although these are rapidly changing, so must be updated to respond to the reality on the ground) recognizing signs of TIP, appropriate actions to take in case of suspected TIP activity, and counseling techniques.

- Education campaigns that target street and other children who would not be reached through school or other community-based programs.

- Community development programs bringing together ethnic and faith-based groups, civil society and families around eliminating TIP in their neighborhoods.

- Youth-oriented awareness campaigns using popular social media. Such campaigns will provide information and confidential referrals on services available to youth at risk for labor and sex trafficking.

- Information campaigns in IDP/refugee camps exposing scam tactics and encouraging residents to report instances of abuse.

- Media campaigns with appropriately reported TIP stories, taking into account the sensitivity of the subject matter, the need for confidentiality regarding the identification of victims, including children, and the avoidance of sensationalism.

*Possible Activity Indicators:*

➢ Percent of target group with increased knowledge of TIP and safe migration practices

➢ Number of public awareness campaigns about TIP completed

➢ Number of specific sub-populations receiving messages tailored to their particular circumstances and vulnerabilities to human trafficking

➢ Number of public awareness campaigns about TIP replicated by host-country government, NGOs, or communities without additional USAID support

➢ Number of schools/teachers using counter-trafficking curriculum

➢ Percent of schools in target area where counter-trafficking curriculum is institutionalized as a regular part of the instructional program

➢ Number of schools/teachers making referrals regarding suspected TIP activity

➢ Number of people in host country trained on TIP-related issues with USG assistance

*1.2.2: Expand economic and educational opportunities for vulnerable populations as alternatives to TIP through:*

- Skills training and vocational education programs tailored to the most economically viable sectors in the region. These programs should be developed in collaboration with local businesses to ensure that participants receive training that will most likely lead to legitimate employment.

- Small business development programs. These programs should include instruction and support in the development of business plans (including market analysis, financial management, marketing strategies, etc.) and be linked to micro-credit lending opportunities.

- Primary education programs, improving the quality of education and creating incentives for parents to enroll and keep girls and boys in school.

- General Education Development programs to improve literacy and basic education.

- Programs designed to expand economic opportunity for populations vulnerable to TIP need to be coupled with TIP education. There have been cases where small loans actually increased TIP; those receiving the loans then used minors in their new small businesses.

*Possible Activity Indicators:*

➢ Number of individuals completing vocational training who obtain employment locally within 3 months

➢ Number of individuals receiving small business support/training who open businesses within 3 months and are increasing their weekly income from that business within 6 months

> Number of vulnerable individuals enrolled in/completing educational programs designed to increase their economic opportunities

> Percentage of vulnerable groups completing educational milestones (primary school, secondary school, GED, vocational school)

> Literacy rate among vulnerable groups

*Measurement Approach:* Vulnerability itself is difficult to measure, but an understanding of the factors that make a specific group particularly vulnerable to trafficking can be used to develop proxy indicators that effectively measure reduction in vulnerability. At the IR level, reduction in vulnerability will likely best be measured by a concise set of indicators that address the most important factors that contribute to vulnerability in that particular country context. For instance, performance indicators relating to a lack of viable economic opportunities or a lack of job skills can serve as proxies for measuring whether vulnerability has decreased. In areas where a lack of understanding of the risks of trafficking contributes to vulnerability, then increased awareness of those risks can be measured. Local organizations working on human trafficking, human rights, child protection, or related areas can serve as excellent sources of information to determine the most vulnerable populations within a given country.

Awareness raising presents its own set of measurement challenges: 1) to what extent did the target group's level of knowledge and/or awareness change as a result of the interventions; 2) whether this knowledge led to behavior change; and 3) to what extent, if any, this behavior change prevented trafficking from occurring. The fundamental challenge at the last stage is measuring something that did not happen.

To address these issues, awareness raising campaigns or social marketing campaigns should be well-researched, based on public opinion and other data sources. Tailored messages that target specific segments of the population and that provide concrete examples of how to avoid/prevent trafficking or access services are the most effective. With this approach, it is possible to conduct impact evaluations of awareness raising campaigns provided that a treatment and control design is planned from the beginning of the intervention.

*Sustainability:* Introducing C–TIP messages into education systems helps ensure that future generations are savvier to TIP schemes, thereby reducing the number of unwitting victims. However, in desperation, people sometimes submit to trafficking situations. Greater impact, therefore, requires the creation of viable economic alternatives. Well-developed public-private partnerships (PPPs) can ensure that programs promoting such alternatives are both more effective and enduring. Local employers benefit from skills/vocational training programs that produce personnel qualified for their employment needs and may therefore support ongoing learning opportunities, such as internships, apprenticeships, and entry-level positions. Governments can provide further incentives for businesses to assume support for such programming through tax credits.

*Special Considerations:* Cultural norms and economic realities may limit the efficacy of education programs in public schools. Girls' education is not emphasized in all cultures, and poverty often causes parents to send their children to work rather than to school. Similarly, written messages on fliers may not reach illiterate and extremely poor people. It is important to consider the geographic reach of radio and television service when considering the use of public service announcements over these mediums. Accordingly, special care should be taken to ensure that the information campaigns reach the target population and are easily understood. C–TIP campaigns can be more effective if they are tailored to a particular audience or region and are informed by focus groups results and high quality survey data. Urban and rural populations often require different types of outreach and messaging.

# Anti-Corruption

## IR 1.3: Corrupt practices that facilitate trafficking reduced

*Issue:* Although corruption permeates the trafficking chain, anti-corruption measures are often a low priority in C–TIP programming. On the other hand, collusion between law-enforcement officials and traffickers, lack of political will and lack of data on TIP-related corruption impedes the implementation of robust anti-corruption programming. Media can play a key role in exposing corruption and reporting on TIP, but it is sometimes hindered in such reporting by a lack of training in investigative journalism, harsh anti-defamation laws, and threats from trafficking syndicates. Effective media training can improve the quality of C–TIP reporting that, in turn, takes into consideration the special needs of victims, including the need for protection from traffickers during legal proceedings. Stories should raise awareness of threats posed by multiple forms of human trafficking.

*Possible Performance Indicators at the IR level include:*

➤ Number of corrupt practices facilitating trafficking whose incidence is reduced[75]

➤ Number of licenses for recruitment agencies and travel/tour agencies (issued, suspended, revoked)

➤ Number of inspections of high-risk businesses to check compliance

➤ Anti-money-laundering risk matrices that look at excessive profits and "red flag indicators" to identify businesses with high potential for engagement in trafficking

➤ Number of exit vs. entry visas

➤ Global Integrity (NGO) country level surveys

➤ Number of safeguards and changes in procedures related to specific targeted corrupt practices implemented

➤ Number of anti-corruption cases filed and/or prosecuted and number of convictions that involved TIP-related corruption offenses

➤ Percent change in attitudes and perceptions about TIP-related government corruption

➤ Reports of missing persons filed in geographic areas vulnerable to trafficking

## Illustrative Activities

*1.3.1: Build capacity of governmental agencies to expose, investigate, and prosecute instances of corruption facilitating TIP through:*

• Helping agencies analyze internal processes to isolate corrupt practices that could contribute to TIP. While many countries have independent anti-corruption agencies, few have specialized

---

[75]This indicator might be measured by formal reassessments of those practices or by surveys of individuals who regularly deal with a particular corrupt practice such as surveying truck drivers who cross borders regularly on how often they are inspected or how often they are asked for bribes. (If only a few corrupt practices are targeted, then indicators tailored to those practices would be appropriate.) Also consider tracking instances of corrupt practices via a blog or reporting portal similar to www.ipaidabribe.com.

training for the types of corruption associated with TIP. Training within anti-corruption agencies will improve investigation techniques specific to the types of corruption that facilitate TIP.

- Establishing TIP departments in Internal Affairs (IA) Units and Offices of the Inspectorate General (OIG). Linking with TIP hotlines (telephonic or via Internet) should be an opportunity to make anonymous complaints/reports of public corruption to the IA Units in law enforcement and OIGs in ministries. Training IA Units and OIGs on investigative techniques unique to TIP cases will help governments install internal checks to identify corrupt practices and isolate corrupt individuals in the field. Special emphasis should be given to governmental entities whose work most closely touches the different aspects of trafficking, including ministries responsible for labor, tourism, immigration, migration, business licensing and regulation, and justice, as well as law enforcement (including border guards). Within USAID, the OIG plays a key role in C–TIP efforts through helping to enforce the Standard Operating Procedures (SOPs).[76]

- Technical assistance to government agencies responsible for facilitating international travel, issuing work permits, registering business entities, and enforcing labor codes. A thorough analysis will identify the primary opportunities for corruption, whether through improper issuance of visas or work permits, failing to properly document transactions, or lax enforcement of labor codes. Steps to minimize discretionary activity by standardizing operating procedures and automating routine functions will help isolate deviations from the norm, which should be investigated for potential abuse of office.

- Incorporate document-tracking systems. Strict controls and documentation of the issuance of official documents, including passports, visas, birth certificates, and business licenses, enhance accountability. Document numbering, official seals, watermarks, dual signature approvals, and other document security systems not only thwart counterfeiters but also help expose public officials issuing fraudulent documents.

- Improve capacity of border and customs agencies to conduct interventions at border, including training, development of risk management profiles, sector specific mapping, and risk indicators for specific situations.

*Possible Activity Indicators:*

➢ Number of corrupt practices facilitating trafficking identified (contextual indicator)

➢ Number of government officials trained on how specific corrupt practices facilitate trafficking, disaggregated by governmental unit

➢ Number of IA/OIG units established or with strengthened capacity to address corruption related to TIP

➢ Number of new anti-corruption investigations into corrupt practices that facilitate TIP opened/completed

➢ Number of government agencies modifying procedures to reduce opportunities for corruption that facilitate TIP

➢ Percent of targeted official documents with strengthened document tracking systems

➢ Number of inspections to ascertain compliance among high-risk entities for trafficking

---

[76]USAID personnel who witness or suspect trafficking are required under the C–TIP Code of Conduct to contact the USAID/OIG at 1-800-230-6539 or 202-712-1023, or via e-mail at ig.hotline@usaid.gov. The USAID Counter-Trafficking Standard Operating Procedure is available at: http://transition.usaid.gov/policy/C-TIP_SOP.pdf.

*1.3.2: Increase transparency of governmental practices related to TIP through:*

- Strengthening civil society's ability to monitor government activities contributes both to exposing and curbing corrupt practices. Legislative, policy, and/or regulatory reform are often needed to liberalize public access to records and court proceedings. Even where the administrative framework is sufficient, the right to access public documents and proceedings often goes unused. Training for civil society organizations on their rights and procedures under freedom of information laws and open meeting laws will lead to greater transparency. Conversely, training for government officers will promote compliance with "sunshine" laws.

- Strengthening media capacity to investigate and report on corrupt practices facilitating TIP. Journalist training on issues specific to TIP and governmental practices that facilitate TIP will improve their capacity to professionally investigate and report on instances of corruption related to TIP. New media designs can be used to engage potential witnesses and gather information, as well as to publicize the outcome of media investigations.

- Supporting e-government or other open government initiatives. Electronic capacity to apply for or update vital documents, register businesses, track international migration, and apply for social benefits not only streamlines the service but also combats corruption by minimizing discretionary authority of civil servants and provides greater access to government information. Electronically recording complaints to police, an anticorruption authority, IA and OIG units, and court cases will enable monitoring efforts to help ensure that appropriate action was taken and isolate deviations of conduct that could evidence corruption.

*Possible Activity Indicators:*

➢ Number of civil society representatives trained on transparency rights and TIP-related corruption issues

➢ Number of reforms to "sunshine" legislation, increasing access to public documents and meetings

➢ Number of members of the media trained on investigating TIP-related corruption issues

➢ Number of e-government applications implemented to increase transparency

➢ Number of whistle blower programs established/supported

➢ Number of witness protection programs established/supported

*Measurement Approach:* As with the incidence of trafficking, it is difficult to measure corruption directly. Measuring the impact on TIP effectuated by the *absence* of corruption is even more challenging. Broad indices published annually, particularly by Transparency International, reflect how perceptions of corruption have changed at the national level. An anti-corruption element of a C–TIP program will likely require a nuanced approach, though the Transparency International score can provide an important contextual indicator.

*Sustainability:* Although reforming public access laws can be an arduous process, once accomplished, it can be difficult to repeal those rights. As NGOs and journalists become accustomed to accessing public documents, attending meetings, and monitoring government performance, efforts by the government to circumscribe those rights would draw scrutiny from citizens and donors alike. Similarly, although automating processes can be expensive and time consuming, once the equipment and programs are in place and people are trained on their use, the resulting efficiencies typically offset the incremental costs of maintaining the equipment. Likewise, effective government control offices (OIGs and IA Units) can be justified by the cost-savings to the state attributed to reduced corruption.

*Special Considerations:* TIP is often a complex, sophisticated and violent form of organized crime. Government complicity is common but can be limited to a few people at various junctures, often in exchange for modest services without a money trail. As such, it can be very challenging to link governmental actors and actions to a TIP scheme. Moreover, threats of violence from a trafficking coalition, or of civil or criminal liability under draconian defamation laws, are strong deterrents for journalists, activists, and even prosecutors working to expose and prosecute public officials facilitating the crime. Furthermore, anti-corruption programming is a sensitive issue for many governments, and addressing TIP too directly through anti-corruption efforts may risk eroding the political will necessary for complementary aspects of TIP programming.

## Demand Reduction

### IR 1.4: The demand for goods produced by trafficked persons or for services provided by trafficked persons is reduced

*Issue:* Increasingly, C–TIP programs are targeting the demand side of trafficking, for commercial sexual exploitation and products resulting from forced labor, in order to reduce the profitability of the crime. Public education campaigns to reduce consumer demand for products in other contexts (e.g., diamonds, ivory) have proven somewhat effective in reducing criminal conduct. Similarly, curbing demand for products of trafficked labor in industries such as agriculture, hospitality, construction, food processing, garments, and commercial sex can reduce the incidence of trafficking.

*Possible Indicators at the IR Level include:*

➢ Average prices for goods/services in targeted industry. (Average price data would typically be obtained by mystery shoppers—individuals hired by an implementing partner to pose as potential patrons and negotiate pricing for a particular standard good or service. This approach can be used in both licit and illicit industries but should be governed by appropriate ethical guidelines.) [77]

➢ Percent of surveyed potential clients/consumers/employers indicating they have changed behavior because of concerns about trafficking

➢ Percent of surveyed potential clients/consumers/employers indicating they are aware of trafficking issues in the targeted industry

**Illustrative Activities**

*1.4.1: Inform prospective consumers of the prevalence of TIP in the production of certain goods by:*

• Posting information at airports, hotels, information kiosks, travel agencies, convention centers, and tourist sites advising visitors of the prevalence of trafficked labor in the production of specific goods marketed to foreigners in particular countries, as identified by the Bureau of International Labor Affairs.[78] Examples include handicrafts, carpets, pirated CDs, and designer knockoffs.

• Supporting broad public education campaigns informing consumers of the prevalence of trafficked labor in the production of goods marketed globally from countries identified by the Bureau of International Labor Affairs in specific product lines, such as garments, jewelry, and shoes.

---

[77]Disaggregate price data by both labor and sex industries.

[78]For listing of goods in countries believed to be produced with trafficked labor, see http://www.dol.gov/ILAB/programs/ocft/tvpra.htm

*Possible Activity Indicators:*

➢ Number of public awareness campaigns about TIP completed

➢ Number of public awareness campaigns replicated by host country governments or NGOs without further USAID assistance

➢ Number of putative consumers reached with awareness messages

➢ Decrease in sales of specified goods in targeted sales markets

*1.4.2: Inform prospective customers/clients of commercial sex workers of the correlations between commercial sex and trafficking through:*

• Informational campaigns advising potential clients of the prevalence of trafficking victims among commercial sex workers. As commercial sex tends to thrive where there are large congregations of men away from their homes, campaigns can target popular tourist and business destinations, installations of military and peacekeeping forces, construction sites, and large sporting events. Accordingly, public information campaigns in conjunction with the hospitality industry, sport associations, security contractors and armed forces, can raise awareness. In addition to reducing demand, informational brochures can contribute to the identification and protection of victims by including information on how to report suspected incidents.

*Possible Activity Indicators:*

➢ Number of public awareness campaigns about TIP completed

➢ Number of public awareness campaigns replicated by host country governments or NGOs without further USAID assistance

➢ Number of consumers reached with awareness messages

➢ Number of VoTs identified through reports from clients/consumers

*1.4.3: Employers proactively raise awareness, prohibit engagement, and promote reporting of suspected TIP activity in industries known to use forced and child labor through:*

• Adoption and implementation of Codes of Conduct for sectors such as hospitality, entertainment, mining, manufacturing, agriculture, and the armed forces. The Codes of Conduct should require those entities to eschew all forms of TIP, provide specific information on fair labor standards and worker rights, and detail procedures for reporting abusive labor practices to law enforcement. Particularly among diplomatic missions, military forces, and multinational corporations and the contractor community, Codes of Conduct should discourage or prohibit the purchase of goods and services affiliated with TIP.

*Possibly Activity Indicators:*

➢ Number of entities incorporating model C–TIP provisions in their Code of Conduct

➢ Number of reportings of suspect TIP activity from entities with C–TIP provisions in their Code of Conduct

*Measurement Approaches:* Directly measuring the effectiveness of efforts to reduce demand for goods produced by trafficked persons is challenging. Measurement at the IR level can focus on the supply side by attempting to look directly at sales trends through an examination of proxies correlated with sales, or on the demand side by collecting data from customers about their likelihood to purchase goods or patronize services. Supply side measures are inherently challenging because of the difficulty of disentangling other causes of changes in sales from the effect of USAID interventions. However, they may serve as an effective complement to demand-side measures.

*Sustainability:* Shaping domestic and global demand by exposing TIP in specific instances creates economic opportunities for manufacturers and service providers that adhere to fair labor standards. To capitalize on the shift in demand, there is a strong impetus for organizations to adopt anti-trafficking messages in their marketing strategies, ensuring consumers of the absence of TIP in their goods and services. Accordingly, donor-supported demand-reduction activities that raise awareness of TIP will eventually be replaced with positive marketing within the private sector, as has been observed with environmental conservation (i.e. advertising use of recycled products and environmentally sustainable production methods), organic foods, and humane treatment of animals.

## Protection

### Development Objective 2: Victim-centered services to provide protection and assistance to trafficked persons and to meet special needs of child victims of trafficking are established and sustainable

The protection of trafficked persons is part of a comprehensive C–TIP response and the cornerstone of a victim-centered approach. According to international frameworks, a trafficked person is entitled to certain rights, including access to a broad range of services and, where appropriate, immigration relief. Comprehensive services necessary to rehabilitation and restoration are best provided through partnerships uniting all relevant stakeholders acting on behalf of victims. The four IRs under this objective focus on the identification of trafficked persons, assistance with return and repatriation for foreign victims of trafficking, the special needs of child victims, and the importance of law enforcement in the protection and assistance of trafficked persons.

### Victim Services

**IR 2.1: System of specialized comprehensive and non-discriminatory services for VoTs established and maintained**

*Issue:* Once identified and released from an exploitative situation, VoTs face obstacles accessing essential services. Services should be accessible to all victims, regardless of age, gender, and immigration status. Trafficked persons are generally in need of housing, medical and psychological treatment, legal services, and economic support, including access to the labor market. However, eligibility for state-supported services often requires that the individual be formally identified as a crime victim and may also be conditioned on cooperation with law enforcement. Even where criminal laws include trafficking, cultural stigma and fear make many victims reluctant to identify themselves as victims. Services, moreover, are often limited to children or female victims of sex trafficking. Finally, survivors without legal residency status may not be allowed to remain in the country to participate in possible criminal proceedings, thereby effectively denying them access to critical services.

*Possible Performance Indicators at the IR level include:*

  ➤ Number of TIP victims assisted by USG programs

- ➢ Percent of identified trafficking survivors who receive two or more services from a suite of comprehensive services
- ➢ Percent of targeted services put in place
- ➢ Qualitative assessment of the scope of services provided
- ➢ Qualitative assessment of the services provided

**Illustrative Activities**

*2.1.1: Develop (or strengthen) and implement systematic procedures to guide first responders (e.g. police, border guards, immigration officials, medical staff and labor inspectors) in victim identification by:*

- Developing (or strengthening) standard interview guidelines and procedures for first responders to facilitate the rapid and accurate identification of trafficked persons. The procedures should consist of uniform standards, conforming to international norms and national standards on victim identification acknowledged by all relevant actors. Social services should not be contingent on cooperation with law enforcement or self-identification.

- Training state and non-state actors most likely to encounter suspected VoTs in victim identification and referral.

- Integrating TIP training into the formal training curricula for health care providers. Training could cover topics such as victim identification, guiding principles regarding provision of care to victims, provision of information to support individual decision-making, handling of sensitive information, and consent-based notification to authorities (such as immigration services or police).

- Establishing and building capacity of a multi-disciplinary task force or other body, linking public and private resources to identify and protect VoTs in accordance with an established identification system. The task force should be part of an NAP and/or be affiliated with the government coordinating mechanism (such as a national referral mechanism (NRM)).

*Possible Activity Indicators:*

- ➢ Development and implementation of standardized interview guidelines and procedures for first responders (Y/N)
- ➢ Number of first responders, healthcare providers and non-state actors trained on TIP issues
- ➢ Number of VoTs identified by trained first responders, as compared to control group
- ➢ Number of actions taken by multi-disciplinary task force (or qualitative review of task force actions)

*2.1.2: Support provision of basic services for survivors of trafficking through:*

- Promoting liaisons and collaboration between government, labor, business, civil society, medical, legal, and cultural circles. In particular, establishing links between law enforcement, immigration and labor officials who identify trafficking cases and civil society organizations that provide care to trafficking victims.

- Maintaining and publishing a current directory of resources available to trafficking survivors and first responders drawing on diverse networks including civil society, media, cultural and religious leaders, hotlines, organized labor, and private channels.

- Establishing a network of licensed safe shelters, equipped to provide appropriate medical, social, and psychological care to survivors in a safe environment. Shelters use a universal, mutually agreed upon case management system and database system.

- Providing basic services (appropriate medical, social, and psychological care) in non-residential locations in multiple locations to male, female, and child victims of all forms of trafficking. (Many TIP victims do not want or need to enter shelters, but still need access to services.)

- Developing (or strengthening) job placement services for survivors. PPPs, tax incentives for businesses that employ survivors, social enterprises, and placement within public service can help on a long-term or short-term basis pending resettlement or repatriation. (Note: Activities that identify TIP victims to employers and fellow employees may not be welcome by some TIP survivors.)

*Possible Activity Indicators:*

➤ Number of shelters/safe houses/non-residential service providers established for TIP victims

➤ Percent of identified trafficking survivors completing intake procedures at official shelters

➤ Number of identified trafficking survivors receiving psychological, counseling or other services

➤ Number of health clinics and facilities which are able to provide care, or refer for care, to meet the needs of trafficking victims and their children

➤ Number of identified survivors obtaining legal residency status (if relevant to context)

➤ Number of survivors receiving (and/or completing) vocational training

➤ Number of survivors retaining jobs in which they were placed for at least 60 days

*2.1.3: Support access to justice for survivors of trafficking through:*

- Training legal aid providers on forced labor and migration issues and the rights and needs of trafficking survivors, including rights on residency, restitution, participation in criminal proceedings, protective services, and repatriation.

- Supporting advocacy efforts to expand survivor protections, including effective restitution policies, residency status for undocumented workers, and witness protection.

- Supporting labor courts for exploited workers to contest abusive working conditions, including forced labor, through administrative proceedings and claims for restitution.

- Supporting legal residency status for survivors pending legal proceedings that allow access to employment and educational and vocational training.

*Possible Activity Indicators:*

➤ Number of legal services providers trained on TIP issues

➤ Number of laws, regulations, and procedures adopted or modified to expand protection of survivors

➤ Number of labor courts receiving technical assistance

*Measurement Approaches:* While measuring service provision tends to be relatively straightforward, there are nonetheless a number of challenges that typically involve the difficulty of obtaining valid, unbiased measurement of the quality of services, since those clients unhappy with services tend to drop out and disappear. It is particularly important to note that survivors who disappear may be significantly different in profile than those who stay for longer periods in shelters and receive more services or for those who receive services from non-residential locations over a longer period of time. The difference in profile is not predictable; those who disappear may be younger or older, from particular ethnic groups, more able to obtain employment and survive in the informal economy, or otherwise different from those who remain behind. This means that data collected from survivors who remain in shelters or who are receiving services from non-residential locations are not representative of the entire target group; such data would tend to have a strong positive bias, rating services more highly since those dissatisfied with services are more likely to leave.

It may still be valuable to collect feedback directly from clients, such as via focus groups, since clients' perspectives are critical in refining and strengthening service delivery. However, such information would not be valid for use in monitoring and evaluation given inherent biases.

*Sustainability*: While survivor needs can be substantial, providing services is essential to both the *protection* and the *prosecution* aspects of combating trafficking in persons. Helping victims obtain legal immigration status in the destination country can help keep them from facing re-victimization in their country of origin. Practice has also shown that viable niches for TIP survivors in the business community exist, and the private sector can contribute significantly to providing victim services.

*Special Considerations:* Distrust of law enforcement, fear of reprisals from traffickers, and social stigma make some victims unwilling to report exploitative actions. Even after trafficking rings have been broken up, ongoing fear and economic necessity may deter survivors from cooperating with prosecutors. Typically, undocumented workers are ineligible for legal employment during the course of legal proceedings. The availability of basic services in destination countries therefore not only helps protect trafficked persons but may also contribute significantly to the prosecution element of TIP programming.

## Repatriation and Reintegration

**IR 2.2: Voluntary repatriation and reintegration processes available to victims of trafficking in line with international standards**

*Issue:* Trafficking victims may be most vulnerable immediately after rescue or escape. Those who have been victimized in a foreign country are often vulnerable to arrest and/or deportation back to their country of origin. Victims of sex trafficking, in particular, may not be accepted back into their communities due to social stigmas. Many have neither the documentation nor the resources to return home and are in a *de facto* state of limbo. Absent repatriation and reintegration procedures complying with international standards, trafficking victims are prone to further victimization and re-trafficking.

*Possible Performance Indicators at the IR level include:*

➤ Percent of changes identified as needed to bring repatriation and reintegration procedures into compliance with international standards completed

➤ Qualitative assessment of degree to which repatriation and reintegration comply with international standards

➤ Percent of recently repatriated trafficking survivors surveyed indicating that adequate provisions had been made for their protection and privacy

**Illustrative Activities**

*2.2.1: Work with appropriate government agencies to develop (or strengthen) and implement rights-based procedures in destination countries to ensure that VoTs are not inappropriately deported to their country of origin by:*

- Supporting legislative reform to criminal law statutes and other relevant legislation to incorporate the definition of "trafficking in persons" in order to ensure that trafficked persons are effectively identified and not deported as illegal immigrants.

- Supporting adoption of legislative or regulatory provisions requiring officials and tribunals responsible for matters relating to illegal immigration and deportation not to proceed with the deportation of a victim while that person is or may be involved in criminal proceedings against alleged traffickers.

- Promoting adoption of repatriation measures to ensure that, when a victim returns to his or her country of origin, provisions are made to ensure his or her protection, privacy, and safety.

- Supporting social marketing campaigns to disseminate information on the promulgation of or amendments to legislation and/or regulatory frameworks to all relevant parties, including law enforcement, court personnel (including judges and attorneys), and others.

- Partnering with immigration services in destination countries and organizations in countries of origin to support and utilize existing voluntary repatriation programs.

*Possible Activity Indicators:*

➤ Number of laws altered to ensure appropriate definitions of "trafficked persons" are in place

➤ Number of cases where a VoT involved in legal proceedings against alleged traffickers is deported

➤ Number of VoTs served by USG supported voluntary repatriation programs

➤ Number of social marketing campaigns informing relevant parties of legislative changes


*2.2.2: Assist countries of origin and destination to mutually employ practices for safe and voluntary repatriation, reintegration, and reunification of trafficked persons through:*

- Developing (or strengthening) a Transnational Referral Mechanism (TRM) that includes relevant state and non-state actors and that sets out procedures for comprehensive assistance and transnational support to VoTs, complementing existing national C–TIP structures and procedures. The TRM should define SOPs for identification, first assistance and protection, as well as the process management of individual trafficking cases, including a rights-based return and/or social inclusion process.[79]

- Establishing domestic rules and regulations regarding responsibilities for repatriation, including training labor attachés in countries of destination on the needs of trafficked persons to ensure their safe repatriation. These rules and regulations should be reflected in the respective government's NAP.

- Establish reunification procedures that enable VoTs to be reunited with their families (such as the T visa model in the U.S).

---

[79] For more information, please see USAID, *Guidelines for the Development of a Transnational Referral Mechanism for Trafficked Persons: South-Eastern Europe* (Vienna: International Centre for Migration Policy Development, 2009), http://pdf.usaid.gov/pdf_docs/PNADS413.pdf.

- Promoting partnerships with civil society, workers' and employers' organizations in both sending and receiving countries to assess the special repatriation and reintegration needs of trafficked persons and to effectively target assistance, including housing needs and opportunities to be financially independent.

*Possible Activity Indicators include:*

➢ Adoption/implementation of a TRM that meets international standards (Y/N)

➢ Number of officials involved in repatriation who receive training on the needs of trafficked persons

➢ Number of civil society, workers' and employers' organizations in both sending and receiving countries involved in partnerships focused on repatriation and reintegration

*2.2.3: Establish reintegration procedures in countries of origin to protect trafficked persons against further exploitation and re-trafficking by:*

- Developing (or strengthening), in partnership with NGOs and government agencies, long-term reintegration plans ensuring that trafficked persons returning to their country of origin receive assistance and support necessary to ensure their well-being and to facilitate their social and economic reintegration.

- Developing (or strengthening) procedures for the safe reintegration of children to ensure safe living conditions, access to education, and the alleviation of risks for subsequent exploitation.

- Working with civil society to form support groups for victims of trafficking to foster mutual support in the return and reintegration process and to improve access to services.

*Possible Activity Indicators:*

➢ Expert panel assessment of long-term reintegration plans

➢ Percent of targeted procedural improvements related to the safe reintegration of child victims of trafficking through adoption

➢ Number of repatriated VoTs participating in support groups

*2.2.4: Support local initiatives that address social and cultural stigmas associated with being a TIP victim by:*

- Developing partnerships with local religious, tribal, and political leaders, and other influential personalities in the local community to raise the awareness of the exploitative nature of human trafficking and the need to reintegrate trafficking victims back into their communities where appropriate.

- Working with trade unions, business associations, civil society and government agencies to develop (or strengthen) community education programs designed to decrease social stigmas associated with being a VoT.

*Possible Activity Indicators:*

➢ Percent of respondents in public opinion survey indicating survivors of trafficking are crime victims, have suffered trauma and need services to overcome the trauma (or believe reintegration after having been trafficked is possible)

> Number of actions adopted by religious, tribal, and other community leaders to support the re-integration of VoTs back into the community

*Measurement Approaches*: Measuring the effectiveness of repatriation and reintegration procedures can include both quantitative and qualitative measures. Quantitative metrics (i.e. number of improved procedures implemented, percent of targeted procedural changes that are adopted) are helpful, particularly when complemented and contextualized by qualitative measures that assess how conducive the legal/procedural environment is to repatriation and reintegration.

In contrast to interventions that provide direct services to trafficking survivors, when working on issues of repatriation, direct data collection methods can be effective. When dealing with repatriation, it may be possible to identify an appropriate sample of repatriated trafficking survivors from whom survey data can be collected. For instance, if survivors are repatriated in groups, questionnaires might be conducted while they are in transit or as they arrive back in their country of origin, allowing them to comment on their experiences with the repatriation process.

*Sustainability:* Relying on employment abroad is an unstable course for national economies. Countries of origin need to have effective macro-level policies to address the root causes of migration that focus on poverty alleviation, employment generation and gender discrimination. Efforts to mitigate punitive deportation and to assist victims of trafficking with successful reintegration in their home countries will become increasingly sustainable as sending and destination countries prioritize long-term rehabilitative care and the creation of viable employment opportunities.

*Special Considerations:* Cultural stigma complicates the potential for successful rehabilitation of trafficked persons. In destination countries, they may be viewed as illegal immigrants taking jobs from the local economy. However, returning home is not a viable option for many trafficking survivors either. If they have been deported and/or convicted of a crime (i.e. prostitution, illegal migration) in the destination country, there may be consequences in their native countries as well. Socially, girls returning from forced prostitution may be ostracized by their communities. Accordingly, activities facilitating repatriation processes must incorporate reasonable safeguards for the victims' return or ensure that other alternatives exist.

## Special Needs of Child Victims of Trafficking

**IR 2.3: The special needs of child VoTs are addressed in a comprehensive victim assistance framework**

*Issue:* The particular physical, psychological and psychosocial harm suffered by trafficked and exploited children require that they be dealt with separately from adults in terms of laws, policies, programs and interventions. Law enforcement officers, social service providers, medical personnel, teachers and other professionals likely to come into contact with trafficked children may lack sufficient training to recognize and assist child victims of trafficking. Once identified, and in the absence of legal guardians, children may be held in immigration detention centers (often in the same facilities as adults) and lack specialized care. Courts often lack the resources or the awareness to provide child victims of trafficking with an appointed guardian or to offer child friendly services for giving testimony.

*Possible Performance Indicators at the IR level include:*

> Percent of identified cases of child trafficking where a guardian/ advocate is appointed

> Average number of services received by identified child survivors of trafficking in target area, disaggregated by type of service

> Percent of identified child survivors of trafficking housed in a designated safe accommodation

- School attendance rate of children designated at-risk of trafficking who are targeted by USG interventions

- Qualitative review of comprehensiveness of services available to child victims of trafficking

**Illustrative Activities**

*2.3.1: Laws and procedures to identify child victims of forced labor and trafficking are strengthened through:*

- Working with civil society, government agencies and parliamentarians to bring national laws in compliance with international standards and definitions relating to forced child labor and trafficking, including the special needs of both girls and boys.

- Partnering with workers' organizations to identify exploited children in the workplace and/or vulnerable children in the community.

- Strengthening the capacity of border patrols and law enforcement officers to effectively screen unaccompanied minors, minors traveling with adults who are not their parents, and other characteristics of vulnerable children.

*Possible Activity Indicators:*

- Percent of identified modifications that are required to bring national laws into compliance with international standards that are adopted/implemented

- Number of workplace mechanisms established that allow workers to report/advise on which members in their workplace or community are vulnerable to exploitation

- Number of individuals identified as vulnerable via workplace mechanisms who receive intervention services

- Number of immigration officers, border patrol agents, police officers, and labor inspectors trained to recognize potential child trafficking situations

- Percent of trained immigration officers, border patrol agents, police officers, and labor inspectors who receive a passing score on a follow-up test 12 months after training

*2.3.2: Facilities and services to effectively address the special needs of child VoTs are established and/or enhanced by:*

- Supporting the coordination of government ministries with responsibilities for children and families, labor, youth, employment, finance, social welfare, law enforcement and education to identify at-risk children and implement policies and programs to prevent children from being trafficked, as well as protect child victims from further harm.

- Strengthening the overall child protection system.

- Working with civil society and government agencies to support the appointment of guardians or advocates to assist children removed from a trafficking situation in accessing services. A guardian could be a trained NGO staff member, a social worker or some other specifically dedicated person. Best practice includes ensuring that the range of appropriate care and legal assistance is provided and that all decisions are in the best interest of the child.[80]

---

[80] UNICEF has developed specific guidelines on the protection of child victims of trafficking, including information on the appointment and related responsibilities of a guardian. For more information, please see UNICEF. 2006.

- Strengthening partnerships between law enforcement officials, civil society and government agencies to ensure referral systems are in place and rapid access to services is available, including safe accommodation, food, medical care, counseling, legal accompaniment, education, and life-skills training.

- Partnering with government agencies and civil society to establish (or improve) safe accommodation for children to avoid detention center placements and to develop (or strengthen) a durable long-term solution to ensure a child's safety and ability to survive.

- Empowering local communities, schools and parent-teacher associations to support the ongoing education of child victims of trafficking and to protect at-risk children by enhancing schools and offering out-of-school activities in cases where children are vulnerable to trafficking. Government subsidies for keeping children in school will help counter the short-term economic obstacles faced by some families. Special focus should be placed on keeping boys and girls in school.

*Possible Activity Indicators:*

➢ Number of actions taken to improve services to prevent child trafficking and serve child survivors as a result of improved coordination of government agencies

➢ Child advocate program established (Y/N)

➢ Number of referrals made through USG-facilitated referral systems

➢ Percent of identified child survivors of trafficking receiving services as a result of a referral

➢ Number of safe accommodation beds for minors established

➢ Number of schools with significant enrollment of at-risk children that receive technical assistance to keep those children, particularly girls, in school

*2.3.3: The legal needs of child VoTs during trials against traffickers are met by:*

- Building the capacity of the judiciary to develop (or strengthen) and implement policies and procedures to protect and assist children in giving testimony, including the involvement of a guardian, use of video testimony, and other means to protect the child and reduce trauma.

- Working with the legal profession to develop (or strengthen) and provide training and workshops for lawyers and legal advocates on the special considerations and legal needs of child victims of trafficking, and all the available remedies to pursue.

*Possible Activity Indicators:*

➢ Number of policies/procedures modified to meet the special needs of child witnesses in trafficking prosecutions

➢ Number of lawyers/legal professionals trained on the special considerations and legal needs of child victims of trafficking, and all the available remedies to pursue

*Measurement Approaches:* Where there are significant numbers of child victims of trafficking identified and referred for services, it is relatively straightforward to measure whether services customized for the

---

*Guidelines on the Protection of Child Victims of Trafficking.* New York, N.Y., 16–17. Also see USAID. 2009. *Guidelines for the Development of a Transnational Referral Mechanism for Trafficked Persons: South-Eastern Europe.* Vienna, Austria: International Centre for Migration Policy Development. http://pdf.usaid.gov/pdf_docs/PNADS413.pdf

---

special needs of child victims of trafficking have been put in place and are being used. Measurement is more challenging where there are relatively few child victims since low numbers make it difficult to discern whether there is systematic improvement.

Another measurement challenge relates to the difficulty of interpreting data on changes in the number of child trafficking cases identified. Police and border control officers who have received training are likely to identify more trafficking cases, but since the total number of undetected cases is unknown, one cannot know whether this is because the total incidence of child trafficking is increasing, or just because enforcement has improved. Similarly, if the number of cases identified decreases, it is difficult to determine if this is because incidence has dropped, enforcement has become more lax, or the traffickers have adapted their methods in response to stronger law enforcement interventions. Accordingly, the total number of identified cases is a contextual indicator rather than an actual performance indicator.

*Sustainability:* Child labor is one of the most heinous forms of TIP, and pressure from the international community on governments to renounce it can be an effective means of sustaining measures to curb child trafficking. Moreover, countries have long-term social and economic incentives to protect their children. Victims of child trafficking are typically uneducated and often physically and psychologically damaged, preventing them from contributing to society in a meaningful way as adults. Governmental subsidies for keeping children in school would help sustain families until the children are able to obtain legitimate long-term employment. Similarly, assistance to child victims potentially prepares them for a productive work life despite the early victimization.

*Special Considerations:* The use of children in the commercial sex trade is prohibited under both US law and the Palermo Protocol—"no exceptions and no cultural or socioeconomic rationalizations preventing the rescue of children from sexual servitude" are permitted.[81] The sale and trafficking of children and their entrapment in bonded and forced labor are among the worst forms of child labor and are treated as trafficking under US law.[82] Children who drop out of school and/or run away from home are often treated as juvenile delinquents and placed in correction facilities. Cultural tolerance of domestic trafficking of children or forced labor within a family further complicates counter-trafficking efforts. Cultural factors also can hamper the care a child receives once removed from an exploitative situation. For example, returning the child to his/her family is not always the preferred solution, as often the family is, or was complicit with the trafficking agent. Yet finding homes for children who should not be returned to their families can be difficult, particularly in countries were child protective services are minimally developed.

## Law Enforcement/Police Interaction

### IR 2.4: Law enforcement entities enhance protection of trafficked persons

*Issue:* A vital aspect of law enforcement is the handling and protection afforded to actual and possible victims of trafficking. Informed law enforcement officers (including immigration officials, border control agents and labor inspectors) are often able to properly identify victims of trafficking and make referrals to services where they exist, avoiding unnecessary detention and deportation. Civil society may be well placed to increase awareness of law enforcement officers on issues involving the protection of exploited and trafficked persons in order to ensure that their rights to protection, confidentiality, legal representation and recourse are upheld throughout the legal process.

*Possible Performance Indicators at the IR level include:*

> Percent of surveyed trafficking survivors rating their initial interactions with police as supportive

---

[81]DOS. 2010. *Trafficking in Persons Report (10th Edition.* Washington, D.C., 12.
[82]Ibid, 9.

---

- Number of referrals by law enforcement of trafficking survivors to appropriate social services
- Qualitative review of law enforcement procedures, training and activity related to protecting trafficked persons
- Percent of surveyed community members in targeted vulnerable communities who view law enforcement as trustworthy links to protection and assistance

**Illustrative Activities**

*2.4.1: Engage law enforcement and local communities to facilitate victim identification and protection through:*

- Increasing the visibility and perception of law enforcement entities as trustworthy links to protection and assistance within immigrant communities, among persons in prostitution, and other vulnerable communities through community outreach activities and the enforcement of anti-corruption measures among local police units.

- Introducing police assigned to work in communities of vulnerable populations, including immigrant communities.

- Promoting joint outreach programs (between law enforcement and local communities) targeting vulnerable populations, including events at orphanages, schools, and within migrant communities.

*Possible Activity Indicators:*

- Percent of targeted vulnerable communities with regular police patrols
- Number of joint outreach programs held that target vulnerable populations

*2.4.2: Develop and strengthen the capacity of law enforcement to assist trafficked persons in accessing social services by:*

- Creating coordination and communication networks among law enforcement entities and civil society organizations that provide services to victims of trafficking. Such networks will provide updated information to law enforcement on available services and points of contact.

- Institutionalizing the representation of law enforcement entities on national and local task forces and coordinating bodies that address issues relating to human trafficking.

*Possible Activity Indicators:*

- Percent of targeted law enforcement personnel receiving briefings on available social services for trafficking survivors. (This should be done for all law enforcement personnel as part of their basic training.)

- Percent of targeted organizations participating in a majority of meetings involving the coordination networks.

- Frequency of updates on available services and points of contact provided by coordinating networks.

- Percent of targeted national and local task forces and coordinating bodies that have law enforcement organizations included as permanent members.

*Measurement Approaches:* Measurement of strengthened law enforcement capacity to enhance the protection of trafficked persons is relatively straightforward. Both quantitative and qualitative indicators can be used to assess whether the actions of law enforcement personnel are more supportive, as well as whether mechanisms have been institutionalized to continue to build that capacity such as training curricula, improved procedures and specialized units and victim advocate personnel.

*Sustainability:* Law enforcement entities are often charged with the procedural task of identifying victims of trafficking, and the cost of training law enforcement to reliably identify victims can be a key investment since they are often the main or even only point of intervention. Moreover, improved communications and processes among government agencies increase efficiency. (It is important to note, however, that if there are very weak vital records systems in the country, establishing identification can be difficult.)

*Special Considerations:* Law enforcement entities have often inhibited identification of victims of trafficking due to a lack of awareness/understanding of trafficking. In some cases, law enforcement has been complicit in the crime. Victims are themselves often unwilling to turn to law enforcement, fearing they will either be reported to the trafficker or incarcerated for illegal migration or prostitution. Accordingly, it is imperative that C–TIP activities both improve the image of law enforcement and increase the understanding of TIP among law enforcement officers and agencies.

## Prosecution

### Development Objective 3: Prosecution of traffickers strengthened, resulting in increased convictions and sentencing

USAID will focus on efforts around prevention of TIP and protection of those who are vulnerable to trafficking and/or those who have been trafficked. The Departments of State and Justice are the USG leads on prosecution. Nevertheless, there are steps that USAID can take to address issues around strengthening justice systems and enhancing witness protection programs before, during and following court proceedings.

**Justice System**

**IR 3.1: Justice systems are capable of effectively, fairly and efficiently handling TIP cases**

*Issue:* Trafficking offenses are difficult to prosecute, conviction rates are low in proportion to the scope of the problem, and criminal sentences are often not commensurate with the seriousness of the crime. Prosecution of these offenses presents difficult challenges: deficiencies in the definition of the crime of trafficking, the frequent need to rely on evidence collected abroad, the potential for victims and witnesses to be traumatized, manipulated, and intimidated, the possibility of corruption among public officials, and the need for interpreters and translators.

*Possible Performance Indicators at the IR level include:*

> ➢ Expert panel review of capacity of law enforcement agencies to investigate TIP cases and of the judicial system to handle them effectively, expeditiously and fairly

**Illustrative Activities**

*3.1.1: Strengthen administrative procedures to promote efficient processing of TIP cases by:*

- Establishing channels of communication between and among local and national law enforcement agencies to ensure prompt and confidential exchange of information.
- Improving law enforcement access to public information, including business records and licensing data, as well as non-public information, as appropriate, in the course of an investigation.

---

- Facilitating information exchange between countries as well as among governmental entities within a country relating to TIP investigations and prosecutions.

- Providing for victim/witness advocates, and/or in the case of minors, a guardian *ad litem*, to ensure the child's rights are respected before and during the proceedings.

*Possible Activity Indicators:*

➢ Number of administrative procedures improved/made more friendly to TIP survivors

➢ Number of victims/witnesses served by advocates or guardians *ad litem* as a result of USG assistance

*3.1.2: Develop (or strengthen) law enforcement's capacity to investigate TIP cases and support prosecution of traffickers through:*

- Introducing modern investigation techniques, including use of the Internet, undercover agents, confidential informants, sting operations, wiretapping, forensic inspection of travel and identity documents, etc.

- Improving evidence gathering skills, including how to interview witnesses (especially children and traumatized victims), how/where to access documentary evidence (including banking, registration, migration, criminal files, phone records, internet communication, etc.)

- Identifying victims of trafficking, and pursuing cases against traffickers rather than arresting victims for prostitution or immigration violations.

*Possible Activity Indicators:*

➢ Number of law enforcement personnel trained in improved investigative techniques with USG assistance

➢ Number of modern investigative techniques introduced as a result of assistance that are utilized in an investigation, disaggregated by whether the investigation results in arrest and prosecution

*Measurement Approaches:* Measuring improvements in the justice system's capacity to effectively, fairly and efficiently handle TIP cases is relatively straightforward. Court records are typically available on arrests, prosecutions and convictions, and in many cases the interventions themselves are relatively straightforward and easily measurable. (In places where this is not the case, e-governance initiatives, as described earlier in the guide, may need to be carried out first.)

There are two major challenges in measuring work in this area. The first is that relatively low numbers of arrests/prosecutions each year can mean that it can take a number of years to begin to see trends, particularly in smaller geographic areas. The second challenge is that there is an absence of information about the extent of the underlying phenomena; no one knows exactly how much trafficking is occurring. It is not clear if trafficking arrests are increasing or decreasing because enforcement is improving or because the amount and/or modality of trafficking is changing; thus indicators need to be standardized in order to be properly understood, e.g. viewed as a percent of arrests leading to prosecution.

Despite these challenges, experimental or quasi-experimental designs that enable a true measure of impact may be possible in some circumstances. Different provinces or courts can be phased into programming and those in later waves can serve as control groups for those who receive earlier assistance. For instance, the percent of trafficking arrests that lead to prosecution/conviction can be measured at baseline across the full set of court jurisdictions due to receive assistance and then rates for those who receive assistance in years 1 and 2 of a program can be compared to those who are not scheduled to receive assistance until years 3 and 4. The challenge with such a design relates to concerns about overall small numbers not allowing enough statistical weight to ensure results are valid, particularly when looking at indicators relating to arrests and prosecutions.

*Sustainability:* International recognition of countries that prosecute TIP helps provide ongoing incentives. Since TIP cases are sometimes hard to identify or isolate in a court docket (as TIP can fall under different charges depending upon the legal framework) creating a specialized unit for prosecution of TIP crimes will help create a high profile means of tracking these efforts. A natural incentive structure for the specialized unit to deliver an acceptable rate of convictions will work to ensure that the investment in capacity building will yield ongoing efforts to prosecute TIP. As the demand for prosecution increases, the demand for better evidence gathering and investigation increases.

*Special Considerations*: In many regions, corruption, incompetence, lack of training, and insufficient resources pervade law enforcement entities. It is common for law enforcement to be complicit in trafficking schemes, to varying degrees. Consequently, efforts to improve the public image of law enforcement will be counterproductive if reality on the ground is at odds with the desired image. Further, investigating and prosecuting TIP cases can be very dangerous for all involved, given the frequency with which traffickers are part of an organized crime syndicate. Training for more proactive investigation and prosecution should be accompanied by consideration for the safety of the individuals involved.

### Support and Witness Protection Programs

### IR 3.2: Safety and protection of trafficked persons institutionalized throughout legal proceedings

*Issue:* Testimony from the victim of a crime is often essential to conviction. Although such testimony may be required to secure a conviction, the act of testifying by a trafficking victim is acutely challenging for that individual for many reasons. A victim may be traumatized, lack sufficient support systems, be unable to understand the language or the process, or feel vulnerable physically, emotionally or financially. Based on their exposure to abuse, isolation, and criminal activities, victim testimony is often inconsistent and contradictory. They may have begun to identify with their abuser, a common coping mechanism under extreme circumstances. Victims do not trust the police or justice system to protect them or their families from reprisal attacks. Accordingly, to promote prosecution of TIP offenses, measures must be taken to build trust and ensure a safer and more secure environment for victims.

*Possible Performance Indicators at the IR level include:*

➢ Number of identified TIP survivors pursuing civil remedies/restitution

Additional illustrative indicators include the following, but may require special caution when applied. See explanation below.

➢ Number of TIP survivors cooperating fully in providing police with information regarding TIP cases

➢ Number of TIP survivors testifying at trial

➢ Percent of TIP survivors who cooperated fully with police who subsequently testify at trial

Caution should be exercised when using the indicators listed above and evaluating the data obtained through these measurements. In many countries, TIP survivors are required to engage in legal proceedings against their traffickers in order to receive any form of support services that may be available to them. In these cases, the extent to which TIP survivors cooperate with police and testify at trial would not be indicative of whether TIP survivors felt their safety and protection were adequately institutionalized throughout the legal proceedings.

**Illustrative Activities**

*3.2.1: Victim rights are protected in the course of legal proceedings by:*

- Supporting public information campaigns to raise awareness of protection services available to TIP survivors engaged in legal proceedings.

- Making suitable housing alternatives available to victims. Holding victims in detention centers further victimizes them. Secure shelters, equipped to meet the physical, psychological, medical and material needs of victims during the investigation and trial makes it feasible for victims to effectively support prosecution efforts.

- Providing victims and witnesses with advocates to protect against harassment or discrimination based on gender, ethnicity, religion, or other factors.

- Promoting evidentiary procedures to safeguard the safety, dignity and well-being of trafficking victims. Protecting witnesses against harassment and intimidation can include shield laws, limiting the extent to which a victim's past sexual or employment history can be admitted. Under appropriate circumstances where essential rights of the criminal defendant are not prejudiced, evidentiary procedures can provide for video-link testimony, witness concealment, or testimony by written transcript. In rare circumstances, a witness's identity can be withheld and hearings closed where undue prejudice to the criminal defendant does not result.

- Incorporating special procedures for taking the testimony of minors balance a defendant's rights to confront witnesses, while protecting the rights of the witness. (See DO2, IR2.3)

- Ensuring security for protection of witnesses in the courtroom, if necessary.

*Possible Activity Indicators:*

➢ Number of trafficking survivors participating in prosecutions who are housed in shelters

➢ Number of shelters/safe houses established for TIP survivors

➢ Number of modifications to laws, regulations or procedures governing evidentiary procedures made to better support the ability of trafficking survivors to participate in prosecutions

➢ Qualitative assessment of degree to which evidentiary procedures support or inhibit the ability of trafficking survivors to participate in prosecutions

➢ Level of awareness among TIP survivors of available legal and protection services

➢ Number of institutions located throughout the country providing services to victims

*3.2.2: Victims are provided for and protected after trial as feasible, through:*

- Developing witness protection programs. After testifying for the prosecution, witnesses and/or their families may be vulnerable to retaliation from affiliates of the traffickers, or the traffickers themselves if they are not convicted and incarcerated.

- Making legal assistance available to pursue civil remedies, or collect entitlements resulting from criminal penalties. Civil cases for past wages, physical and emotional damages are often available, though TIP survivors will likely need legal assistance to pursue these remedies. In addition, victims may require legal assistance to claim restitution from criminal penalties.

- Enforcing limitations on the disclosure of information concerning the new location of the victim. In balancing the public's interest in information against the risk and privacy rights of victim witnesses, care should be taken following a criminal proceeding to avoid disclosing contact information or location of prosecution witnesses.

*Possible Activity Indicators:*

➢ Number of trafficking survivors receiving witness protection

➢ Number of trafficking survivors receiving legal assistance to pursue civil remedies/ restitution

*Measurement Approach:* Measurement approaches for this IR will focus on monitoring changes in the way trafficking survivors are treated during legal proceedings. As with other elements of improving prosecution, it can be difficult to effectively capture these changes because of the relatively low number of legal proceedings that occur in most jurisdictions, which makes it difficult to identify trends. Another challenge involves the difficulty of obtaining information from TIP survivors who stop participating in legal proceedings.

In particular, it is important to be careful in using measurement methods that require direct data collection from groups of survivors about their treatment during prosecution since those survivors who drop out (and are thus not reached in the survey) may be different in profile from those who persist through to the end of prosecution. Focus groups or data collection from survivors who make it through the prosecution process can be tremendously helpful in identifying additional ways to strengthen the system, as can having shelter staff or victim advocates keep records of the reasons cited by survivors who drop out of prosecutions. Such methods are typically not quantifiable for use in measuring performance indicators, though they certainly can provide important contextual insight.

*Sustainability*: Witness protection activities are expensive and therefore not particularly sustainable. However, some of the most important protections can be incorporated as a matter of evidentiary procedure, including shield laws and alternatives to live testimony. Once adopted, these procedures are eminently sustainable as they require little investment. Moreover, many of the other protections are a matter of adopting a victim-centered approach, and require little more than a civil and professional demeanor. Finally, many countries have legal aid services, which could accommodate victim claims with only marginal incremental costs.

*Special Considerations:* Providing care and security for victims of trafficking during the investigation and lead up to trial can drain limited resources. This could deter prosecutors from bringing all but the most serious TIP cases to trial. Moreover, protecting witnesses following the trial is prohibitively expensive for all but the wealthiest countries. Even where funding exists, relocation and creation of a new identity is often unsatisfying for the victim.

## Partnerships

### Development Objective 4: A global movement dedicated to the eradication of TIP collectively and productively supported by governments, civil society, and the private sector

Successful efforts to combat TIP require effective and efficient coordination across a broad range of stakeholders. Partnerships and coordinating bodies need to focus on bringing together local, national and regional networks. These bodies need to be comprised of representatives from all relevant government agencies, civil society organizations, media, universities, labor unions, and the private sector. Partnerships can be useful in developing long-term C–TIP strategies and in monitoring and reporting on TIP. The four IRs under this development objective focus on coordinating national government, civil society, and private sector C–TIP efforts; improving the collection, analysis and sharing of reliable data; and enhancing regional collaborative initiatives.

## National Coordination

### IR 4.1: NAP and/or NRM coherently coordinate C–TIP activities

*Issue:* As a crime of opportunity, effectively combating TIP requires sustained commitment to *prevent* future occurrences, *protect* victims, and *prosecute* perpetrators. Growing the movement inside any specific country will necessarily involve coordinated action among ministries responsible for education and the economy, social services and health, as well as interior, foreign affairs, labor, immigration, and justice. Civil society, student groups, media, and the private sector also play critical roles in collaborating with national and local governments. Consequently, C–TIP activities are more sustainable and effective if conducted pursuant to a coherent NAP and/or NRM that is implemented and overseen by a competent and accountable coordinating mechanism.

*Possible milestone indicators might include:*

➢ NAP and/or NRM completed
➢ NAP and/or NRM officially adopted by the government
➢ National coordinating body constituted
➢ Mechanism to exchange information among local and national bodies, as well as other diverse stakeholders established
➢ Hotline established

*Possible qualitative indicators might include*

➢ Expert panel rating of quality of NAP and/or NRM
➢ Rating the effectiveness of national coordination against a checklist of observable best practices. (The checklist might include additional elements such as whether civil society representatives are included; whether a survivor is included; or rating how much a single individual or small group dominates discussions.)

### Illustrative Activities

*4.1.1: Develop (or strengthen) a comprehensive NAP and/or NRM drawing on current data and reasonably conceived to combat TIP through sequenced and coordinated activities by relevant stakeholders premised on:*

• An initial assessment of the nature and scope of the problem as well as the enabling factors. The assessment will help define the vulnerable population, identify remedial actions, and justify budget allocations supporting recommended interventions.

• An implementation plan, with firm timelines for specific activities and designating responsible entities. To measure impact, the implementation plan should include intermediate and long-term goals and designate the method for tracking progress towards those goals at regular intervals. It is important that cost associated with implementation of the plan be estimated.

• Defined standard operating procedures that outline the roles and responsibilities across government and non-governmental entities to ensure comprehensive assistance and support to trafficked victims. Protocols may include identification, first assistance and protection, longer-term assistance and social inclusion, reintegration and return, and criminal and legal proceedings.

• A budget, allocating reasonable funds for each activity, and designating the source of those funds.

- Stakeholder input. Throughout the development (or strengthening) of the NAP and/or NRM, stakeholder consultations will promote good will and help ensure future collaboration from critical contributors within the government, civil society, media and private sector.

*Possible Activity Indicators:*

➢ Percentage of NAP progress milestones completed on schedule

*4.1.2. Establish and/or build the capacity of a coordinating mechanism to review performance of an NRM or oversee implementation of the NAP by:*

- Ensuring that the coordinating mechanism has adequate authority. Activities foreseen in NAP and/or NRM will require cooperation and action of high-level officials. Consequently, the coordinating mechanism must be vested with sufficient authority to set priorities and compel action from the various governmental actors involved.

- Establishing accountable and open systems. Given that corruption is a key enabling factor in TIP, safeguards need to be incorporated to ensure that the coordinating mechanism is fully accountable. A dual reporting structure will help maintain objectivity and insulate against improper influences from senior officials. An additional layer of scrutiny comes through systematically engaging stakeholders at open meetings where use of funds and status reports are presented for substantive input.

- Providing adequate resources and capacity. As the entity responsible for overseeing implementation of the NAP and/or NRM, the coordinating mechanism will need to be able to evaluate the impact of interventions and make policy recommendations in response to changing needs. Moreover, public relations and coalition building will be essential functions within the coordinating mechanism.

- Requiring that the coordinating mechanism solicit local input. The NAP and/or NRM should reflect the knowledge, experience, and promising practices of local actors involved in protection, prevention, and prosecution.

*Possible Activity Indicators:*

➢ Number of national coordinating body meetings held per year
➢ Average attendance at meetings, disaggregated by type of group
➢ Number of national coordinating body members trained

*4.1.3: Promote effective implementation of the NRM and/or NAP through:*

- Diverse C–TIP stakeholders (NGOs, government entities, donors, etc.) meet regularly to coordinate efforts.

- A national C–TIP free hotline is established and staffed with trained social workers who can refer victims to appropriate assistance, help investigate reports of TIP, and provide educational information.

- Empirical data collected and analyzed, providing sound guidance for C–TIP activity.

- SOPs followed, ensuring timely identification of VoTs, and provision of appropriate services and protection.

- Reasonable budget allocations for C–TIP activities.

*Possible Activity Indicators:*

➢ Number of stakeholder coordination meetings per year

➢ Number and quality of social workers trained to operate hotline

➢ Number of instances of successful follow up (VoT identification, services provided, TIP case filed) to hotline tips

➢ Number of institutions using empirical data on TIP

*Measurement Approach:* In assessing progress on national coordination, there are two key questions of interest at the IR level: a) are the necessary actions occurring and b) is the quality of the process and product conducive to long-term collaboration and success. Simple milestone indicators will typically suffice to measure much of the first, third and fourth indicators while qualitative indicators will typically be required to offer significant insight on the second.

*Sustainability:* International pressure provides incentives for countries to demonstrate political will to address TIP. The Council of Europe's Group of Experts on Action against Trafficking in Human Beings (GRETA) monitors member state adherence to the Convention on Action against Trafficking in Human Beings, recommending remedial action as necessary. Similarly, the DOS Annual TIP Report assesses country compliance with the TVPA and carries the threat of sanctions for countries not deemed to be making good faith efforts to meet the TVPA standards. Furthermore, the correlation between TIP and other forms of organized crime, notably drug trafficking, provides further incentive for countries to adhere to their NAP.

*Special Considerations:* C–TIP programming is inevitably politically sensitive for affected countries, some of which do not acknowledge the existence of the problem. Moreover, conclusions in the various international TIP reports are highly contentious and subject to criticisms of bias and inconsistent methodologies. Governments in denial and antagonized by the conclusions and threats in the international TIP reports are less likely to exert the political will necessary to establish NAPs or make coordinating mechanisms effective. The lack of funding provided to implement NAPs and/or NRMs often poses the greatest challenge to addressing TIP. For instance, almost all countries in the E&E region have such plans with responsible government entities identified, but the lack of funding impedes the adoption of concrete actions. Effective monitoring of the extent to which the NAP or NRM is being implemented can also be hindered by diffusion of responsibility across government entities, lack of capacity to effectively monitor, and lack of political will. Civil society organizations may be able, in some cases, to fill this gap and to provide the type of information that is needed to assess progress under the NAP or NRM.

## Data Collection

### IR 4.2: Reliable data on TIP activity is effectively collected and shared among interested governmental and non-governmental parties

*Issue:* C–TIP activities should be premised upon reliable and consistent data concerning the nature and scope of the problem in a specific locale and over time. Political sensitivities, however, often cause countries to deny or underestimate the extent of TIP within their borders. This problem is compounded by the absence of vital records and other source documents, especially for those most vulnerable to TIP (IDPs, impoverished children, refugees, etc.) The lack of common definitions of TIP used in data collection and coding, combined with the inherent difficulty of measuring illicit conduct has resulted in substantial discrepancies within and across data systems. Maintaining the confidentiality of victims poses serious challenges, which can also restrict or block access to the data. Although challenging to create and maintain, cross-border databases can improve the tracking of VoTs by following them across borders.

*Possible Performance Indicators at the IR level:*

➤ Government produces TIP estimate annually

➤ Percent of international best practices in data collection implemented in government's annual approach to collecting TIP data

**Note:** This indicator would be measured by annual review of the government's data collection process against a checklist of best practices developed at the beginning of the project.

➤ Percent of governmental and non-governmental organizations, including academic institutions, successfully accessing national TIP database on at least one occasion

➤ Effective case management systems institutionalized, tracking cases across the entire sequence of case measures

**Illustrative Activities:**

*4.2.1: Build host country capacity to measure the incidence of TIP through:*

- Birth registration programs. Unregistered children are at a higher risk of being trafficked; it is harder to trace their disappearance. Moreover, in many countries, unregistered children cannot attend school. Information campaigns should inform parents of the importance of registering their children, as well as the procedures for doing so. Those campaigns should also reinforce the message that registration leads to education which can lead to economic advancement. Technical assistance can help governmental agencies streamline processes and reduce the cost of issuing vital documents. In some countries a complete restructuring and/or development of vital records may be required. Outreach programs to outlying areas and streamlining the process in hospitals and orphanages will make birth registration more accessible to vulnerable rural populations. Improved mechanisms for ensuring that vulnerable populations can easily and routinely obtain vital documents should be institutionalized. This process can be expensive in certain contexts. Special efforts may be needed to reach minority groups that may be unlikely to register the birth of their children (for example, the Roma in the E&E region).

- Improved vital document systems. Documentation of migrant workers, IDPs, refugees and children is necessary to quantify the vulnerable population and provide a baseline that will help estimate "disappearances" that may be a result of TIP.

- Standardized data collection protocols. Instituting uniform standards governing the collection of qualitative and quantitative data on arrests, convictions, rescues, escapes, repatriation, and social and medical services related to TIP will promote the reliability, accuracy and comparability of data among different agencies and over time. Disaggregation by gender, ethnicity, and age will increase the comparability of data across jurisdictions.

- Trained personnel. Government officials responsible for data collection, including law enforcement, medical and social service providers, court personnel, and immigration officials must be trained on the protocol, standardizing when and how specific data is collected and to whom it is reported. Moreover, responsibility for data collection within the government will ideally be assumed by a central C–TIP coordinating mechanism.

*Possible Activity Indicators:*

➤ Number of officials trained on the collection of TIP data

➤ Percent of targeted first responder agencies submitting data on schedule

- Percent of population for whom baseline data exists regarding education, residency, and employment

- Number of individuals obtaining vital documents, such as birth certificates, as a result of USG assistance

- Number of adults in IDP or refugee camps registered as a result of USG assistance

- Percent of target population covered by improved, institutionalized mechanisms for obtaining vital documents

*4.2.2: Improving the integrity and the utility of TIP data through:*

- Creation of an integrated database. The coordinating mechanism should include a data collection function that assimilates data from multiple sources, including law enforcement agencies and social service providers, local NGOs, and international experts. In many countries, multiple, non-interfaced databases are created and maintained by different entities. These diverse systems are often partial and competing. The challenge in such cases is establishing a single, integrated system. Models comparing data from different sources and tracking correlations will help analyze impact and refine future programming.

- Improved access to data. Agencies responsible for implementing the NAP/NRM must have timely access to pertinent data to adapt their activities strategically. For example, service providers will be better able to prepare for demand with access to reliable data on the size of vulnerable populations and models estimating the percentage likely to be victimized by traffickers, and border patrol agents with access to data on the vulnerable population will be better informed of likely victim profiles. Moreover, academic and research institutions should play an active role in the collection, verification and analysis of TIP data.

*Possible Activity Indicators:*

- National TIP database established (Y/N)

- Percent of targeted information system improvements

- Number of analytic and/or statistical reports produced by national reporting agency

- Universities and/or research institutes publish timely reports on TIP dynamics and trends based on data analysis

- Universities and/or research institutes provide innovative approaches and methods to C–TIP community

*4.2.3: Develop (or strengthen) formal mechanism to share TIP data with relevant entities within and across national borders through:*

- Institutionalizing protocols (ideally through a TRM) that enable information to be shared with all concerned entities within and across national borders. The system to exchange information should enable process management of individual trafficking cases and cover the entire process, from victim identification, assistance and protection, participation and support during legal proceedings and legal redress, to return or resettlement of the trafficking victims in their destination, origin, or third country.[83] The protocols should ensure the protection of personal data and privacy of the victims.

*Possible Activity Indicators*

➢ Transnational data sharing protocols institutionalized (Y/N)

➢ Referral and case management data available to authorities on a transnational basis (Y/N)

➢ Percentage VoTs identified in other countries, for whom case files exist

*Measurement Approach:* The key to measuring the effectiveness of the government's measurement efforts at the IR level is focusing on both whether measurement mechanisms are in place and being used, and also on the quality of those mechanisms.

*Sustainability:* Incorporating standard protocols into the daily routines of officials in various government agencies helps ensure that the practice will be ongoing. Moreover, an attempt to retract the policy of making this information public and shared internally among agencies would result in unsatisfied demand from civil society and policymakers. Finally, international C–TIP organizations, including the UNODC, the Council of Europe, and the Organization for Security and Cooperation in Europe, have emphasized the importance of reliable and consistent data collection. This effort may encourage countries to develop comprehensive data collection processes.

In building a measurement system, collaboration with researchers at a top university will reduce costs and build indigenous capacity. A well-trained PhD-level social scientist in sociology, political science, criminology or public health should be able to design an appropriate data system.

*Special Considerations:* Data collection systems confirming the extent of TIP within a country can lead to difficult results for national governments. Similarly, reporting agencies have incentives to produce numbers that portray their institutions in a positive light, which may lead to inconsistent data—i.e. prosecutors want to report high convictions, border patrol agents want to report low incidence rates, police want a high correlation between arrests and conviction, etc. Assurances from high-level governmental officials may help guard against reporting agencies skewing numbers.

There are a number of special considerations in building databases of this type. One must balance the need for multiple entities to have input with the privacy and confidentiality needs of the victims. Data may need to be encoded or case numbers assigned to protect identities. Using a system of this sort requires sufficient training and vetting of people with access to the database to make sure that they will use the data correctly. The ICMPD has compiled a handbook on data collection and the use of such databases.[84]

## Regional Cooperation

**IR 4.3: Legal and voluntary mechanisms supporting international, intergovernmental and regional collaboration and partnerships to combat TIP are adopted and utilized**

*Issue:* The weak capacity of the State to enact and enforce laws often results in a culture of impunity and an unregulated labor market where TIP flourishes. Partnerships involving governments, international

---

[83]USAID. 2009. *Guidelines for the Development of a Transnational Referral Mechanism for Trafficked Persons: South-Eastern Europe.* Vienna, Austria: International Centre for Migration Policy Development. http://pdf.usaid.gov/pdf_docs/PNADS413.pdf, 8–9.
[84]http://www.ungift.org/doc/knowledgehub/resource-centre/ICMPD_Handbook_on_Anti-Trafficking_Data_Collection_in_SEE.pdf

---

agencies, civil society and business can work to augment C–TIP efforts by amplifying messages and leveraging resources for an effective and sustainable response, thereby accomplishing more together than any one entity could alone. The primary conventions, protocols, memoranda, joint actions, recommendations, and declarations serve as important frameworks for governments to define the types of interventions necessary given the country context.

*Possible Performance Indicators at the IR level include:*

➤ Number of relevant international and regional instruments ratified by target country

➤ Number of relevant international and regional instruments with strengthened utilization

➤ Number of TIP survivors repatriated facilitated under the auspices of cross-border collaboration mechanisms

➤ Number of programs initiated by PPPs to strengthen compliance with labor standards and number of firms reached by those programs

➤ Value of donations from corporations or other donors involved in PPPs to efforts to prevent trafficking and protect survivors

## Illustrative Activities

*4.3.1: Generate support for ratification of relevant international instruments through:*

● Support to civil society, trade union and business efforts to encourage parliamentarians to ratify applicable international and regional instruments without reservations, including the Palermo Protocol and ILO Conventions on the elimination of forced labor and child labor. Efforts might include advocacy campaigns, roundtables, workshops and media outreach.

*Possible Activity Indicators:*

➤ Number of advocacy campaigns supporting ratification of relevant international and regional instruments with USG support

➤ Percent of supported advocacy campaigns followed by formal action toward ratification within 12 months of campaign

*4.3.2: Build government capacity to implement international instruments, setting minimum standards and responsibilities through:*

● Assistance to legislative bodies to conduct Legislative Impact Analyses (LIAs) for conventions prior to ratification. Many conventions do not allow reservations and must be implemented in full upon ratification. LIAs are therefore necessary to identify and resolve any conflicts with national law and policy.

● Building the capacity of government ministries (labor, judiciary, health) to comply with the reporting requirements of international and regional instruments, to administer national and local programs, and to actively respond to observations and recommendations from various monitoring reports.[85]

● Supporting compliance with international and regional instruments. This requires the establishment of procedures for victim identification, protection, repatriation and return, as well

---

[85]Relevant monitoring reports include the DOS TIP Report, the DOL List of Goods Produced by Child Labor and Forced Labor, GRETA, and recommendations from the ILO's supervisory bodies.

as criminal proceedings involving trafficked persons. It includes also knowledge-sharing and capacity-building workshops to develop/strengthen such procedures and involve government officials from pertinent ministries, researchers, social partners and other interested stakeholders including international partners.

*Possible Activity Indicators:*

➢ Number of LIAs conducted with USG assistance

➢ Number of host country government officials trained on issues related to complying with international treaties and regional agreements

➢ Number of host country agencies demonstrating improved compliance with international treaties and regional agreements

➢ Percent of international and regional instruments that include reporting requirements for which the target country government reports accurately and on time

➢ Number of monitoring reports to which the host country government responds effectively in accordance with international norms

*4.3.3: Support the development (or strengthening) of internal, cross-border and regional networks to facilitate awareness raising, identification, care, repatriation and reintegration, cross-border investigations and services by:*

• Building the capacity of international C–TIP networks to facilitate identification of victims, cross-border investigations and prosecutions, and repatriation and resettlement.

• Supporting international and domestic monitoring systems to increase pressure on governments to adhere to obligatory reporting requirements under relevant conventions and protocols in instances of trafficking involving transit to other countries.

*Possible Activity Indicators:*

➢ Number of cross-border and regional counter-trafficking networks established

➢ Number of individuals involved in counter-trafficking networks trained on trafficking issues

➢ Number of compliance monitoring reports issued

*Measurement Approach:* Measuring the establishment of key counter-trafficking infrastructure such as mechanisms supporting collaboration is relatively straightforward. Measuring the quality, utilization and efficacy of these mechanisms is less so.

*Sustainability:* In addition to international conventions, Member States can apply pressure to noncompliant neighboring states to adhere to the standards and meet reporting responsibilities. Accordingly, technical assistance to build domestic capacity to comply with reporting requirements and implement minimum standards will be continually reinforced under the scrutiny of the international community.

*Special Considerations:* Ratification is typically a lengthy process and requirements that are more stringent than domestic standards deter many countries. Even those interested in participation will find the process of reconciling domestic laws with the convention's standards politically demanding and time consuming. Nonetheless, countries can adopt counter-TIP measures even as the ratification process is underway.

---

## Public-Private Partnerships and Intragovernmental Partnerships

**IR 4.4: Establishment of partnerships between both public and private entities and within the USG**

*Issue:* C–TIP is not something that can be done within the vacuum of legislation and court proceedings. Robust C–TIP efforts require a wide variety of partners coming together around a common purpose. Partnerships between public and private entities allow for a wider audience to be reached in efforts to raise awareness about TIP. Moreover, partnerships within the USG (i.e. USAID partnerships with SOCOM, CENTCOM and AFRICOM) can help integrate TIP throughout the planning processes of all agencies. USAID is committed to growing a global movement to raise awareness of TIP and consolidate C–TIP efforts of all stakeholders—including governments, civil society, private businesses, and consumers.

*Possible performance indicators at the IR level include:*

➢ Number of new stakeholders (public and private) actively pursuing C–TIP activities

➢ Public attitudes towards TIP reflect increased demand for action by governments

**Illustrative Activities**

*4.4.1: Support PPPs and promote CSR initiatives to combat TIP by:*

- Facilitating PPPs that emerge from a shared interest to prevent the use of child and forced labor in the supply chain of production. Given the reputational damage to companies not monitoring their supply chain for trafficked labor, PPPs have an incentive to proactively exercise greater vigilance to ensure that supply chains are TIP-free.

- Facilitating multi-stakeholder initiatives developed through the coordination of civil society, trade unions, companies, and governmental bodies that work to promote good business practices and comply with labor standards throughout their supply chains.

- Encouraging business alliances that promote codes of conduct within an industrial sector (i.e. agriculture, construction, textiles).

- Initiating and institutionalizing donor dialogues and coordination. USAID's investments should be leveraged by partnerships with public and private donors.

*Possible Activity Indicators:*

➢ Number of PPPs facilitated with USG assistance that raise awareness among consumers about trafficking or monitor the use of trafficked labor in the supply chain

➢ Number of business alliances formed to address TIP within an industrial sector

➢ Number of donor dialogues resulting in C–TIP investments

*4.4.2: USG collaboration strengthened internally to combat TIP by:*

- Strengthening the civilian and military collaboration on TIP in terms of country and regional level planning. This can happen with the relevant COCOMS, and it should also happen with DOD representatives present in individual countries.

- Building upon existing collaboration between multiple members of the USG in C–TIP efforts to ensure USG commitment to C–TIP is visible, coordinated and effective.

*Possible Activity Indicators:*

➢ Number of USG coordination meetings held per year

➢ Average attendance at meetings, disaggregated by types of group

*Measurement Approach:* In assessing progress on partnerships (both public-private and internal USG) there are two key questions of interest at the IR level: a) are the necessary actions occurring and b) is the quality of the process and product conducive to long-term collaboration and success. Simple milestone indicators will typically suffice to measure much of the first, while qualitative indicators will typically be required to offer significant insight on the second.

*Sustainability:* Incorporating standard protocols into the daily routines of officials in various government agencies helps ensure that the practice will be ongoing. Moreover, an attempt to retract coordination efforts would result in dissatisfaction within the USG.

*Special Considerations:* USG is promoting a cohesive and concerted global movement against TIP. This requires making C–TIP a priority throughout the USG, incorporating it into programming, and joining forces with other stakeholders. Growing this movement will require collaboration on bilateral, regional, and global bases as well as across all stakeholders. This poses challenges for donor organizations that typically work on bilateral bases to incorporate regional outlooks and complementary programming.

# Annex H. Health Care and Human Trafficking

Trafficking victims are exposed to both physical and psychological harm. Health care providers can play a vital role in helping to ensure that trafficked individuals receive health care in a safe and confidential environment. Moreover, health care providers can play a vital role in victim identification. In many cases, a health care provider who may suspect that a given health issue is the result of trafficking offers the first opportunity for a victim to be identified. It is therefore important that health care providers are actively involved in coordinating mechanisms that link victims to legal and protective services and other community resources.

Like victims of torture, individuals who have been trafficked may experience a range of symptoms and signs. TIP-related illnesses and injuries vary according to individual circumstance, gender, age, and type of exploitation, whether sexual or labor related. These include, but are not limited to, physical health problems, mental health problems, dental trauma, injuries or illness related to sexual abuse such as STIs, including HIV/AIDS, substance abuse, and illnesses associated with crowding, poor nutrition, and poor hygiene. In addition, occupation related health problems can result from repetitive use injury, exposure to chemicals and toxins (the skin, lungs, nervous system, gastro-intestinal tract), and muscular-skeletal strain.

The children of trafficking victims and child trafficking victims may experience additional and specific health issues; they may lack basic primary health care (such as immunizations), be anemic or malnourished, and have poor personal hygiene. In some cases, the children of trafficking victims have also witnessed trauma inflicted on the parent or caregiver. (See Section IR 2.3 on the special needs of the child victim of trafficking.)

As important as care of victims, health care providers should be aware of the potential dangers and risks to their own staff and take necessary precautions for their physical safety and for infection control at the health center. Health care providers should be prepared to alert security staff if imminent dangers arise in service provision to the victim.

Health care providers should accurately document any findings or reports generated during the care of the trafficked person. Those records should be kept in a secure place and remain confidential unless released by the victim. The ethics principles of beneficence, informed consent and patient autonomy, non-maleficence, and justice (non-discrimination) should also be respected in the provision of health care.

# ANNEX I. ADDITIONAL RESOURCES

## Prevention and Protection

- The *Training Manual to Fight Trafficking in Children for Labour, Sexual and Other Forms of Exploitation: Understanding child trafficking,* produced by ILO, UNICEF, and UN.GIFT, aims to equip users with a broad and comprehensive understanding of child trafficking. It is intended for use by governments, workers' and employers' groups, NGOs, and international agencies working on behalf of children. http://www.unicef.org/protection/files/CP_Trg_Manual_Textbook_1.pdf

- *UNODC's Toolkit to Combat Trafficking in Persons* offers specific strategies to prevent and combat trafficking in persons, to protect and assist victims, and to promote international cooperation. It is intended for policymakers, law enforcement officials, judges and prosecutors, victim service providers and concerned members of civil society. http://www.unodc.org/pdf/Trafficking_toolkit_Oct06.pdf)

- *UNICEF's Guidelines on the Protection of Child Victims of Trafficking* set out standards for good practice with respect to protection of and assistance to trafficked children. The guidelines are based on international human rights instruments and look at the protection of trafficked children from their identification through recovery and integration. http://www.unicef.org/ceecis/0610-Unicef_Victims_Guidelines_en.pdf

- The Office of the High Commission for Human Rights commissioned a study on challenges and best practices in the implementation of the international framework for the protection of the rights of the child. http://www2.ohchr.org/english/issues/migration/consultation/index.htm

## Service Provision

- *USAID's Methods and Models for Mixing Services for Victims of Domestic Violence and Trafficking in Persons in Europe & Eurasia* considers service models for victims of trafficking in persons and domestic violence in the Europe and Eurasia region. In particular, the study focuses on how and where services may be mixed and where services should be distinct, as well as where additional services are required to meet the needs of victims of domestic violence or human trafficking.http://www.usaid.gov/locations/europe_eurasia/dem_gov/docs/dvtip_mixed_services_final_020909.pdf

- A Handbook on Justice for Victims of Crime and Abuse of Power was developed by UNODC as a tool for implementing victim service programs and for developing victim sensitive policies, procedures and protocols for criminal justice agencies and others who come into contact with victims. Section two of the Handbook provides detailed useful and relevant material on implementing victim assistance programs. http://www.unodc.org/pdf/crime/publications/standards_9857854.pdf

## Referral Mechanisms

- *OSCE's National Referral Mechanisms: Joining Efforts to Protect the Rights of Trafficked Persons: A Practical Handbook* includes several useful questionnaires that can be used for an assessment of the human trafficking situation in a given country. Questionnaires cover

---

assessment of country-specific conditions and needs, legal frameworks, and actors and organizations. http://www.osce.org/odihr/13967

- *USAID's Guidelines for the Development of a Transnational Referral Mechanism for Trafficked Persons: South-Eastern Europe* contain a comprehensive set of measures to be taken by C–TIP stakeholders in order to ensure effective and safe transnational referral of trafficked persons. They promote the concepts of government ownership, civil society participation and multi-disciplinary approach as a prerequisite for a sustainable and comprehensive national C–TIP response. http://pdf.usaid.gov/pdf_docs/PNADS413.pdf

## Monitoring and Evaluation

- *An Evaluation Framework for USAID-Funded TIP Prevention and Victim Protection Programs Final Report*, intended for USAID staff and implementing partners, is designed to help users understand what is involved in evaluating anti-TIP program impact and to provide specific suggestions when planning evaluations. http://pdf.usaid.gov/pdf_docs/PNADR431.pdf

- *IOM's Handbook on Performance Indicators for Counter-Trafficking Projects* is a resource and guide for project managers, developers, implementers, evaluators and donors working in the field of counter-trafficking, who want to develop performance indicators for their counter-trafficking projects.http://www.iom.int/jahia/webdav/shared/shared/mainsite/published_docs/brochures_and_info_sheets/pi_handbook_180808.pdf

## Health

- *Caring for Trafficked Persons: Guidance for Health Providers* produced by UN.GIFT, IOM, and the London School of Hygiene & Tropical Medicine provides valuable information for healthcare providers on how to offer culturally appropriate, individualized care to victims of human trafficking. http://publications.iom.int/bookstore/index.php?main_page=product_info&products_id=510

## Partnerships

- The United Nations Global Initiative provides a good framework for business alliances, work with all stakeholders to support each other's work, create new partnerships and develop effective tools to fight TIP, including a training manual on trafficking in children. https://www.ungift.org/ungift/en/stories/launch-of-training-manual-to-fight-trafficking-in-children.html

- The UN Global Compact is a strategic policy initiative for businesses that are committed to aligning their operations and strategies with ten universally accepted principles in the areas of human rights, labor, environment and anti-corruption, including the elimination of child and forced labor. http://www.unglobalcompact.org/

- Advocacy campaigns can be bolstered by participating in annual global events that recognize international standards, such as the World Day Against Child Labor. http://www.ilo.org/ipec/Campaignandadvocacy/WDACL/WorldDay2010/lang--en/index.htm

- Partnerships between the non-profit sector and the private sector can accelerate action against trafficking in persons and forced labor. These partnerships take many forms. The Better Work program is a partnership that brings together employers, workers, and governments to improve labor standards compliance in global supply chains. http://www.dol.gove/ilab/highlights/if-20100727.htm and http://www.betterwork.org.

- All nonimmigrant visa holders in the U.S. receive a "Know Your Rights" pamphlet during their Embassy interview that outlines their rights and how to get help if these rights are violated. http://www.travel.state.gov/pdf/Pamphlet-Printer.pdf

- The DOL's International Labor Affairs Bureau produces two publications of use: List of Goods Produced by Child Labor or Forced Labor http://www.dol.gov/ilab/programs/ocft/PDF/2011TVPRA.pdf, designed to increase awareness of the problem of child and forced labor among governments, consumers and industry; and, "Prohibition of Acquisition of Products Produced by Forced or Indentured Child Labor Reports," otherwise known as Executive Order 13126 Reports. These documents require the Department of Labor, in consultation with the Departments of State and Homeland Security, to publish and maintain a list of products, by country of origin, which the three Departments have a reasonable basis to believe, might have been mined, produced or manufactured by forced or indentured child labor: http://www.dol.gov/ILAB/regs/eo13126/main.htm